PADRAIC WOODS

30 IRISH ADVENTURES

MERCIER PRESS

WHAT YOU NEED TO READ

MERCIER PRESS

Cork

www. mercierpress. ie

Trade enquiries to CMD Distribution
55A Spruce Avenue, Stillorgan Industrial Park,
Blackrock, County Dublin

ISBN: 978 1 85635 587 2

10 9 8 7 6 5 4 3 2 1

Dedication

For my family

A CIP record for this title is available from the British Library

Mercier Press receives financial assistance from the Arts Council/An
Chomhairle Ealaíon

Printed and bound in the EU

Acknowledgements

In writing this book I've been lucky enough to see parts of Ireland I had never seen, to meet some of the most interesting people I've ever met and to try new and exciting adventure activities while sharing the whole experience with friends and family. This book began with an inspirational kayaking journey to a magical island in West Cork with two of the most active people I know. My sister Siobhan and her husband Enda. This book would not have been possible without their boundless help and support throughout the year.

I would particularly like to thank Siobhan for helping me write this book, for the long hours she spent proof reading each chapter and for inspiring me to write the book in the first place. I'd like to thank all our friends and family who accompanied Siobhan and I throughout Ireland; Lee, Brian, Dennis, Shelly, Sheila, Pauline, Aongus, Marc, Helga, Ole, Ed, Rob, Donal, Mrs. O' Regan, students from St Vincent's School in Cork and our family. It's not easy writing an Irish travel book while living in another country. The past year has involved borrowing cars, bikes, boats, houses, beds, fishing gear, surf boards, wet suits, snorkelling gear, being picked up from the airport and dropped off again. Thanks to everyone who has helped me out along the way. I would like to thank all of the activity providers mentioned in the book for sponsoring the activities and for sharing their infectious enthusiasm for their activity.

Safety

All adventure activities involve an element of risk. The adventure activities in this book were carried out by people experienced in the activity or under the guidance of experienced guides. If you are interested in trying one of the activities in the book contact one of the clubs or activity providers listed about taking a lesson. Many of the clubs and organisations provide group insurance schemes covering injury.

1.	Rock Climbing, Dalkey Quarry, Co. Dublin
2.	Paragliding, Mount Leinster, Co. Wexford
3.	Snowboarding, Irish Ski Club, Kilternan, Co. Dublin
4.	Wakeboarding, Summerhill, Co. Meath
5.	Cycling, Slieve Bloom Mountains, Co. Laois
6.	Canoeing, River Barrow, St. Mullins, Co. Carlow
7.	Kitesurfing, Dollymount Strand, Co. Dublin
8.	Hillwalking, Spinc and Glenealo Valley Route, Glendalough, Co. Wicklow
9.	Hillwalking, Howth Head, Co. Dublin
10.	Coaststeering, Hook Head, Co. Wexford
11.	Sea Kayaking, Castleisland, Co. Cork
12.	Bodyboarding, Garrettstown, Co. Cork
13.	Sea Kayaking, Sandycove, Co. Cork
14.	Surfing, Co. Sligo and Co. Clare
15.	Whale Watching, Union Hall, Co. Cork
16.	Mountain Biking, Balyhoura, Co. Limerick
17.	Moonlight Sea Kayaking, Kinsale, Co. Cork
18.	Snorkelling, Kilkee, Co. Clare
19.	Hill Walking, Carrauntoohil, Co. Kerry
20.	River Walking, Kilfinane, Co. Limerick
21.	Horse Trekking, Achill, Co. Mayo
22.	Hill Walking, Achill Head, Co. Mayo
23.	Sailing, Lough Ree, Athlone, Co. Roscommon
24.	High Ropes course, Killary Adventure Centre, Leenane, Co. Galway
25.	Wind Surfing, Rusheen Bay, Co. Galway
26.	Hill Walking, Croagh Patrick, Co. Mayo
27.	Caving, Belcoo, Co. Fermanagh
28.	Blokarting, Nutts Corner, Co. Antrim
29.	Mountain Boarding, Mourne Mountains, Co. Down
30.	Cycling, Antrim Coastline

CONTENTS

ROCK CLIMBING

DALKEY QUARRY CO. DUBLIN

We met with our guide, Garry, on a sunny September morning in the car park of Dalkey quarry. We booked a one-day rock climbing course for three beginners. Garry began by outlining the aims for the day; to climb and abseil lots of routes, to learn movement and climbing techniques, knot tying, belaying, safety procedures and, most importantly, to challenge ourselves. Garry gave each of us a harness and helmet and wasted no time in setting up a safety rope from the top of our first climbing route, 'Paradise Lost', a grade VD (Very Difficult). The basic Irish and UK grading system describes the overall difficulty of the climb. The grades are Very Difficult (VD), Severe (V), Hard Severe (HS), Very Severe (VS), Hard Very Severe (HVS) and Extremely Severe (E1, E2, E3 …).

Very difficult is the entry grade for most beginners and 'Paradise Lost' is often the first route new beginners take in Dalkey quarry.

The nerves settled as Garry explained all the climbing equipment used and how the safety rope was set up for the first climb. The first climb began from the quarry floor; one person climbed the route while another learned to belay from the ground (bottom roping) under Garry's supervision. The belayer is responsible for removing any slack from the safety rope attached to the climber; this insures that a climber falls no more than the slack available. All three of us flew up this relatively easy route, using the time to perfect our knot-tying and belaying technique.

With the confidence up we quickly moved on to our second route, 'Yorkshire Pudding', a grade HS (Hard Severe). Garry set up the safety ropes on this new route as before by anchoring the rope onto two metal anchors and tree trunks. This time we began by abseiling down the route. Abseiling is the technique of descending down the rock face using a fixed rope; it's often considered more dangerous than climbing as the rope takes your full weight for a long period. The first step off the cliff face was a heart stopper – learning to trust the equipment is a big part of climbing. Abseiling was a great buzz; I only wished that the rock face was higher. Abseiling involved self-belaying down the rock face while using your legs to bounce off it. After a break for lunch we decided to climb back up the same route.

'Yorkshire Pudding' has two crux moves (the hardest move on the climb). The climb felt a lot easier than our first climb until I reached the two crux moves. It took a lot of guidance from Garry to find the appropriate hand and foot holds to get past these tricky spots. You have to rely on natural rock holds; there are no bolts or man-made crevices. There is a strict 'no bolting' policy in Dalkey quarry and, indeed, much of Ireland. Sports climbing involves the use of bolts (fixed metal protection which is permanently bolted to the rock) and is generally frowned upon in Ireland. 'Traditional' climbing (climbing using traditional forms of protection, i.e. nuts, etc.) is possible in most places as the rock allows for the placement of temporary protection, and because this is always removed there is no environmental damage. The routes were definitely getting harder and all three of us were looking forward to our final climb of the day.

The last route was called 'Street fighter' a grade VS (Very Severe). Looking up at this seemingly flat rock face we tried to map out a possible climbing route. Garry led the climb and secured the safety rope to the top of the quarry as before. The first climber failed to make it past the crux move; with exhausted arms and legs he called it a day. The next climber made it all the way, struggling only on the crux move. I was the last man up. I got past the crux move and was within two metres of the top. Clinging on to the rock face by your fingernails up a 10-metre rock face wondering where you are going to place your next hand or foot delivers a real adrenaline rush. My forearms were burning and my legs started to shake – that's why they call it the 'Elvis' move. I couldn't see where my next move was going to be and I was starting to make bad excuses about big feet and small holds. Garry guided me to a handhold from the bottom and I was soon touching the top of the quarry. A simple shifting of your hand or foot a couple of inches can make a big difference when rock climbing.

Climbing is as much about mental strength and pure stubbornness as physical ability; it is very easy to talk yourself down from a climb. The reward and sense of achievement are therefore huge when you manage to overcome your fears and physical exhaustion to conquer the climb.

Getting there:

By Car: Dalkey is 26 km from Dublin airport and 12.8 km from Dublin city centre; simply follow the signs for Dun Laoghaire ferry terminal from the city centre and all approach roads to the city. Take the coastal road south-bound past the Dun Laoghaire ferry terminal, following the signs for Dalkey.

From Dalkey village follow the signs for Killiney, taking the Dalkey Avenue Road uphill. Turn left onto Burton Road; at the end of this road is the Killiney Hill car park. The quarry is located northeast of the car park.

Train:

Dalkey is easily accessed from Dublin city via the DART (Dublin Area Rapid Transit) train service. The journey takes about thirty minutes from the city centre DART station on Tara Street travelling south (www.irishrail.ie). Dublin Bus number 8 leaves from Parnell Square and takes about an hour to Dalkey (www.dublinbus.ie). You can also take the number 59 bus from Dun Laoghaire.

The area:

Dalkey quarry is one of Ireland's best rock climbing sites. The disused granite quarry is located within the Killiney Hill park, a small public park overlooking Dalkey village to the north. On a clear day there are spectacular views of Dublin city to the northwest, the mountains of Wales to the east and southeast and Bray head and the Wicklow mountains to the south.

The quarry is divided into four sections. The highest cliffs are on the upper tier just below the old signalling tower on top of the hill. Far east, east and west valleys are at a lower level, separated from the upper tier by a flat plateau. The far east valley is private property and closed to climbing but the east and the west valleys contain numerous accessible climbs. The Irish Mountaineering Club's guidebook to Dalkey quarry lists about 300 climbs, with climbing grades up to E7 (Extremely Severe 7). There are climbs to suit all abilities. These valleys can be accessed via a path from the plateau to the Ardbrugh Road entrance to the quarry.

Provider:

Climbing courses vary in price and length, but average prices are between €60 and €100 per day. I took a one-day beginners' course with Garry Rossiter of Adventure Agency Ireland (www.adventure.ie). The course covered all safety aspects and took in four different climbs. It lasted from 10 a.m. to 4 p.m. and cost €80. All equipment was provided.

A list of BOS (Bord Oiliúint Sléibhe /Irish Mountain Training Board) certified courses, centres and prices can be found on the Mountaineering Council of Ireland (MCI) website (www.mountaineering.ie).

Take plenty of water, warm clothes, some food and, ideally, a pair of climbing shoes or, alternatively, light runners with a good grip.

More about Rock Climbing:

Ireland's geology features a variety of different rock types, ranging from the hard granite cliffs in Dalkey to the softer limestone found in the Burren.

Some of the most popular climbing areas in Ireland include Dalkey (near Dublin), Glendalough, 47 kms south of Dublin, Fair head in Co. Antrim, Muckross head and Gola Island in Donegal and the Burren in Co. Clare. Climbing is becoming more popular in Ireland, mainly due to the increase in the number of indoor climbing walls providing short climbs in a safe and weather-protected learning environment.

For a comprehensive list of climbing sites in Ireland, see www.climbing.ie.

You should never attempt to climb unless you have been fully trained or are being supervised by someone experienced or trained to do so.

There are two main climbing shops in Dublin: The Great Outdoors (located just off Grafton Street) and The Outdoor Adventure Store (Abbey Street). Both give a 10 per cent discount to MCI members.

The Mountaineering Council of Ireland (www.mountaineering.ie) has a comprehensive list of mountaineering clubs and organisations in Ireland. The list contains clubs that participate in both hill walking and rock climbing.

Accommodation:

Dalkey is only thirty minutes by DART from Dublin city centre. For a comprehensive list of accommodation options in Dublin, see www.visitdublin.com or contact the Dublin tourist office from within Ireland at (1850 230 330) or from outside Ireland at (+353 (0)66 979 2083). For accommodation options in Dalkey, see the accommodation section on www.dalkeyvillage.com.

Other attractions:

The nearby village of Sandycove is the home of the James Joyce museum. The British originally built the small Martello tower, which houses the museum, as a defence against the expected Napoleonic invasion. It was here that Joyce stayed while writing the first chapter of the novel, *Ulysses*.

Dalkey Island, located 300 metres from Coliemore harbour, is a small island comprising 9 hectares. From the mainland you can clearly see a Martello tower and the ruins of St Begnet's church. The fishermen at Bulloch harbour can bring you out to the island for a small fee.

Dalkey Castle and Heritage Centre (www.dalkeycastle.com) offers guided walks of the centre during the summer months, with actors giving an animated account of the history of the village.

Killiney beach, a short walk from Dalkey quarry, is a stony beach frequented by locals during the summer.

Best time to go/season:

Spring to autumn. There are plenty of indoor climbing walls to practise on during the winter months.

Links:

www.dalkeyhomepage.ie,
www.dalkeyvillage.com,
www.mountaineering.ie,
www.climbing.ie,
www.rockclimbing.com,
www.fairheadclimbers.com.

PARAGLIDING MOUNT LEINSTER, CO. WEXFORD

Our classroom sat on top of Mount Leinster, and as our instructor, Fred Lahif, presented our introductory lesson to paragliding we looked over the green valleys of Carlow and Wexford below.

This was the first lesson of a Para Pro 1 course, which is the first of five stages of becoming a proficient paraglider. Fred went through the basics of wind currents, uplift from the mountain, safety techniques, equipment, landing, launching and how different mountain shapes produce different wind currents. He explained the need for patience when taking up the sport of paragliding as a lot of time is spent parawaiting, the act of waiting for the right conditions to paraglide. Fred makes it clear that 'if you don't have the time to dedicate to paragliding then this sport is not for you'. A lot of days are wasted waiting for the right conditions to get off the ground. The positive side of parawaiting is the social aspect; paragliding seems to attract a diverse range of people who you can't help but get to know when waiting hours on end for the weather to change.

On the day a strong wind and heavy cloud cover hampered our efforts. Fred explained that paragliders below a Para Pro 3 grade should not fly in such conditions. Some of the more experienced paragliders took their gear out to test the conditions. A few got off the ground and, much to our envy, were soon soaring high above us. By mid-afternoon the winds had started to die down and the cloud cover had disappeared. However, the wind was still too strong to practise launching the canopy so Dave (an instructor) took each Para Pro 1 student on a tandem flight.

Dave's passion for paragliding is infectious. Last year he spent six months paragliding his way around South America with the canopy in his backpack. He described his adventures as we made our way onto the mountainside carrying all the paragliding paraphernalia. Dave explained that the wind was still too strong to launch but with a bit of luck and a lot of patience it would die down long enough for us to get off the mountain. He laid out the canopy and strapped on the seat harnesses. While testing the wind strength he explained that we wouldn't try to take off in anything over 15 knots. We waited on the mountainside for about twenty minutes before noticing a shift in the weather, when the wind turbines on a nearby mountain started to change direction. Dave took a last wind strength reading before giving the go-ahead. My job was simple; when Dave said 'go' I was to take two and a half steps down the mountain before taking off, then slip the paragliding seat under my ass and sit back and enjoy the view. Everything went to plan and we were soon off the mountain. We were only a couple of metres above the ground, moving quite quickly along the mountain ridge. If we didn't gain height quickly we would end up 'bottoming out'. 'Bottoming out' is when you can't get enough lift off the ground and you end up flying straight down to the foot of the mountain. I couldn't imagine anything worse after all the parawaiting I'd been doing. A pressure device called a variometer started to beep loudly, indicating we were in a thermal and on the way up. Thermals are columns of rising hot air that paragliders take advantage of to gain height. We then began soaring above the mountain ridge, gaining height with each turn. The view was spectacular and the feeling exhilarating.

We circled the mountaintop for another forty minutes in a constant search for thermals, taking in the amazing views of the valley below before gently touching down. My job on touchdown was to simply put one foot slightly forward and gently step down on the ground. Everyone should get a chance to experience this bird's eye perspective of the world. Soaring effortlessly in a silent glide while your dangling feet frame the landscape hundreds of feet below is simply breathtaking.

I have definitely caught the paragliding bug and can't recommend it highly enough.

Getting there:

Paraglide Ireland run training courses from different training sites. The site chosen will depend on the weather conditions on the day of your course. You will be notified of the meeting place prior to the first day of the course. The most common meeting place is the main street in Blessington, Co. Wicklow. Blessington is located 20 km south of Dublin on the N81 road. All students must make their own travel arrangements to and from the training sites. You will need a car to access the majority of training sites.

Site A: Black Hill (commonly known as Lacken) is located on the east side of Blessington reservoir above the village of Lacken.
Site B: Lough Bray is located at the lower of the two corrie lakes at the top of the Glencree valley at the back of Kippure mountain.
Site C: The Nine Stones, located below the TV transmitter on Mount Leinster in the Blackstairs mountains, Co. Wexford.

open valleys are perfect for hang gliding and paragliding.

Provider:

Paraglide Adventure Ireland

Contact Fred Lahif: (+353 (0)87 258 9245; +353 (0)1 830 3884) www.paragliideadventure.com (Paraglide Adventure Ireland is a registered trading name of Blokart Ireland Ltd)

There are five stages of paragliding proficiency. The first introductory course, Para Pro 1, costs €700. The course consists of learning to perform your daily inspection of equipment and pre flight checks, and learning to inflate, control and inspect your paraglider while you are still on the ground. This is followed by a minimum of ten short top-to-bottom gliding flights from one of the training sites in the Wicklow mountains. The Para Pro 1 course will take a minimum of three trainable days to complete.

Bring light windproof clothing, ankle supporting boots, a packed lunch, plenty of water and a camera.

For information about tandem flights contact Dave Donnelly (+353 (0)86 308 1729).

More about Paragliding:

Paragliding originated in Europe in the early 1980s when a group of parachutists decided to run off the steep Alp slopes at Mieussy in France with their ram-air canopies inflated over their heads. Using a canopy designed for parachuting, they managed to follow the con-

The area:

Mount Leinster at 796 metres (2,605 ft) is the highest hill in the Blackstairs mountain range. The Blackstairs mountains form a natural boarder between Counties Wexford and Carlow. A road barrier at the nine stones car park restricts road access up to the peak of Mount Leinster where a distinctive TV transmitter stands. The rolling hlls surrounded by

tour of the mountain down to the foot of the mountain, and so paragliding was born. Since then the equipment has rapidly improved, allowing paragliders to soar in the air for hours, climb to high elevations and fly long distances across country.

The governing body of the sport of paragliding in Ireland is the Irish Hang Gliding and Paragliding Association (IHPA). The IHPA promotes hang gliding and paragliding throughout the country and looks after the interests of its members. There are currently over eighty registered IHPA members in Ireland. The IHPA organises competitions and fly-ins around the country on most holiday weekends, and many members regularly fly and socialise together whenever the weather is suitable. On completion of each Para Pro course all documentation, along with verification from your instructor, is sent to the IHPA training officer, who will then issue you with the appropriate proficiency rating.

Any student wishing to take up the sport of paragliding should join the IHPA and take advantage of the reduced annual membership on offer to those enrolled on one of the courses. For all students taking a Para Pro 2 or Para Pro 3 course it is mandatory to be a paid up member of the IHPA.

There are five stages in the Para Pro rating system:

o Low gliding flights. (Don't fly higher than you care to fall.)
o Higher altitude gliding and multiple-choice exam. (Altitude and space to manoeuvre, no soaring.)
o Basic soaring and multiple-choice exam. (Soaring in non-turbulent conditions.)
o Advanced soaring. (Soaring in turbulent conditions.)
o Cross country

The time taken to complete a course largely depends on the weather conditions and the students' ability and flexibility to paraglide whenever the conditions are favorable. For more information about paragliding in Ireland check the association's website, www.ihpa.ie.

Accommodation:

For accommodation in the south east of Ireland check out the accommodation section on www.discoverireland.ie/southeast.aspx or contact the Carlow(+353 (0)59 9131554, www.carlowtourism.com) or Wexford (++353 (0)53 9161155, www.wexfordtourism.com) tourist offices.

Other attractions:

The Blackstairs mountains offer plenty of hill walking possibilities. The Barrow Towpath, the South Leinster Way and the Barrow Way walking trails all pass nearby. The South Leinster Way (102 km) and the Barrow Way (113 km) are two long-distance signposted walking trails and part of the national way-marked walking routes (www.walkireland.ie). Fishing and canoeing on the nearby river barrow (see chapter: Canoeing - River Barrow ,St. Mullins, Co Carlow).

Best time to go/season:

Paragliding is very weather-dependent. The wind strength and prevailing weather on any given day will dictate whether flying is possible. In favourable conditions it is possible to fly and train at any time of the year. However, in winter the days are shorter and bad weather can curtail all flying activity for long periods. The main flying and training season in Ireland runs from March to the end of September as this is when the weather is usually at its best. Paraglide Adventure Ireland also run training trips abroad where weather conditions tend to be more stable, allowing the paraglider to undertake a number of training flights in a short time period.

Links:

www.ihpa.ie (Irish Hang Gliding and
Paragliding Association),
www.paraglideadventure.com,
www.fai.org (The World Air Sports Federation),
www.met.ie (Irish weather service).

SNOWBOARDING
IRISH SKI CLUB,
KILTERNAN, CO. DUBLIN

I have been snowboarding for years but never on an artificial dry slope; I was excited about comparing the dry slope against the real thing. The slope in Kilternan ranks among the finest dry slopes in Europe, boasting a 180-metre main slope, two nursery slopes, a 130-metre intermediate slope and two ski lifts. The slope is covered in thick bristle netting that's kept lubricated by a regular spray of a fine mist of water. This allows for year-round skiing and snowboarding on a fast, flowing surface.

We arrived at Kilternan two days before Christmas to an unexpectedly quiet ski slope. The Ski Club of Ireland is run by the voluntary efforts of its members. This includes office personnel, instructors and a maintenance team. Three instructors took three different groups with varying snowboarding experience out on

the slope. I had brought along my younger brother to take a first-level beginners' lesson. There were four beginners in his group, three of whom wanted a crash course in snowboarding before travelling abroad on a snowboarding holiday. Each boarder was given ass padding, boots and a snowboard fitted to their preferred standing position. If you prefer to stand with your left foot forward it's called a regu-

lar stance, right foot forward is called a goofy stance. Cian, a very patient instructor, took the four snowboarders through the essentials of snowboarding. He quickly demonstrated **boot** and board bindings, the proper body position and, most importantly, how to fall. He explained that snowboarders spend a lot of time on their ass, especially when learning. The next **two** hours were spent learning heel-side edge and

toe-side edge start and stops and how to turn. By the end of the lesson all of the snowboarders managed to snowboard the short beginners' slope without falling. Cian explained that 'if you can snowboard on the artificial slope you will have no problem on snow'.

Having snowboarded before, I had full access to the two main slopes for a three-hour practice session. There were only five other snowboarders on a practice session, leaving plenty of room on the slopes and the luxury of no ski lift queues. The two main slopes are short straight runs with little variation. The more

adventurous boarders set up jumps along the slope and were pulling off impressive stunts on this unforgiving surface. I used the time to work on improving my technique before finishing off with a few top-to-bottom speed runs. I was surprised at how much fun the dry slope was and at how hard the surface was when you fall.

Dry slopes can never compete with the real thing. They do, however, allow beginners to learn the basics and the more experienced skiers and snowboarders to perfect their technique. Another considerable advantage is that the slope opens year-round and conditions don't really vary. Learning to ski on an artificial surface gives invaluable experience for people going on their first ski holiday.

Getting there:

The Ski Club of Ireland is situated in the grounds of the Kilternan Golf and Country Club (currently being rebuilt) on the R117 between Kilternan and Enniskerry. Leave the M50 at exit 15 and follow the signs for Kilternan. At the T-junction at Palmers pub in Kilternan turn left. Continue straight ahead for approx. 2 km. The slopes are visible from the road. Follow the signs for the car park.

The 44C bus stops outside the entrance to the ski club. For an updated bus timetable, see www.dublinbus.ie

The Area:

Kilternan is a small village located at the foot-hills of the Dublin mountains in south County Dublin. The green fields of Kilternan are disappearing rapidly as land in the area is being developed for residential property. Kilternan boasts both a ski club (www.skiclub.ie) and a golf club (www.kilternangolfclub.ie).

Provider:

The Ski Club of Ireland is a non profit-making organisation dedicated to the promotion and development of the sport of skiing in Ireland through the provision of classes to all standards from complete beginner to expert.

The Irish Ski club offer classes for skiers and snowboarders of all abilities from beginners to advanced. The slopes are available for practice to competent skiers and snowboarders. The ski club organises weekday classes

Ski and Snowboard Tuition Rates:

	Non Member	Member	Season Ticket Holder Course of four classes
Adult	€150	€135	€75
Student	€135	€99	€67
Under 18s	€100	€85	€55
One class			
Adult	€45	€40	€22
Student	€40	€29	€20
Under 18s	€30	€25	€15
Practice Session Rates (3 Hours)			
Adult	€33	€28	FREE
Student	€28	€23	FREE
Under 18s	€25	€20	FREE

More about Snowboarding:

Snowboarding began in the United Stattes in the 1960's but only became a winter Olympic sport in 1998. Snowboarding originated when a surfer called Sherman Poppen built a surfboard for the snow in 1964. The idea was improved upon by Dimitrije Milovich and Jake Burton (founder of Burton snowboards) in the 1970's and 1980's. Today snowboarding is big business with numerous snowboard manufacturers, professional snowboarders and high-profile competions such as the winter X-Games, the US Open and the Olympic games. The most popular snowboarding style 'freestyle' encorporates man made features such as rails, half-pipes, and quarter-pipes.

along with weekend and full-day 'learn to ski and snowboard' courses. There are two types of classes for children: kindergarten (aged four to seven years) and regular children's classes. Check www.skiclub.ie for course times and other information.

Wear warm flexible clothing, strong gloves and long socks. Scarves are not allowed on the slope. Classes go ahead in all weather conditions. Skis, snowboards, boots, poles are provided at no extra cost.

The club organises a number of ski club holidays each year. You must be a ski club member to book a place on an organised group holiday.

For more information see www.skiclub.ie
Phone: +353 (0)1 295 5658
Email: sci@skiclub.ie

Accommodation:

For accommodation near Kilternan try The Cottage B&B (+353 (0)86 846 2450) located only a short distance from the slope; Sandycove Guesthouse, Dun Laoghaire (+353 (0)1 284 1600); Ulysses Guesthouse, Bray (+353 (0)1 286 3860); Brides Glen farmhouse B&B, Shankill (+353 (0)1 282 2510), Marina House hostel, Dun Laoghaire (+353 (0)1 284 1524, www.marinahouse.com) or Bewleys hotel, Leopardstown (+353 (0)1 293 5000, www. bewleyshotels.com). Kilternan is located only a short distance from Dublin city centre. For a comprehensive list of accommodation options in Dublin check the www.visitdublin.com website or contact the Dublin tourist office from within Ireland at (1850 230 330) or from

Other attractions:

Situated on the Dublin–Wicklow border, the Kilternan Ski Club is a short drive from the famous beauty spots of Co. Wicklow, and just twenty-five minutes from the attractions of Dublin.

The nearby Wicklow mountains are popular with walkers (www.wicklownationalpark.ie) and mountain bikers (www.madmtb.com). Local attractions include Ireland's highest waterfall at Powerscourt Estate and Gardens, Enniskerry (www.powerscourt.ie), Ireland's highest pub, Johnnie Fox's (www.jfp.ie), famous for their food and Irish traditional music, and Leopardstown racecourse (www.leopardstown.com).

Best time to go/season:

The ski club season lasts from September to April. The slopes are open for practice skiing and instruction classes from Monday to Friday from 7.30 p.m. to 10.30 p.m. and on weekends from 10.30 a.m. to 5.30 p.m.

Ski classes on weekdays start at 8 p.m. and finish at 9.30 p.m. Classes on Saturdays start at 11 a.m. and 3 p.m. and Sunday classes start at 11 a.m., 2.30 p.m., 3 p.m. and 4 p.m.

If you are taking a class you must be at the ski club thirty minutes before the class starts to get fitted out for equipment.

Links:

www.skiclub.ie; www.kilternan.info.

WAKEBOARDING
SUMMERHILL, CO. MEATH

Wakeboarding is a relatively new sport in Ireland, combining elements of water-skiing, snowboarding and surfing techniques. As with water-skiing, the boarder is towed behind a speedboat or a fixed cable at speeds of between 16 and 24 mph. More experienced riders use faster speeds with longer ropes. The rider wears a single board with stationary bindings, standing sideways as on a snowboard or skateboard. Wakeboards are shorter in length than snowboards and slightly wider. Boats designed specifically for wakeboarding typically have larger wakes than water-ski boats.

We arrived at the Irish Aquatic Sports Centre in Summerhill on a September morning. A long driveway leads up to a magnificent log cabin overlooking a man-made lake. A manicured lawn and lake stand on what was once a stone quarry. After digging out the quarry, a natural spring was discovered which filled the lake with water. The lake itself is quite small, but large enough for wakeboarding.

We met with Gavin and Éamonn, who run the Irish Aquatic Sports Centre. Éamonn is the world disabled wakeboarding champion and Gavin has competed for Ireland in inter-

national wakeboarding competitions. Gavin prepared the board and boats while we put on our wetsuits.

Like all other board sports you need to first decide on your stance. A goofy stance is right foot forward and regular stance is left foot forward. Two of us had booked a one-hour lesson; I had wakeboarded a couple of times before and my friend was a complete beginner. The lesson began with us squeezing our feet into the tight bindings and dropping from the back of the boat into the water. Gavin explained that the hardest part of learning to wakeboard is the start. The key, he explained, is to relax your body and let the boat take you out of the water rather than you trying to pull yourself out. It should be noted that being pulled out of the water is considerably easier

using the sidebar. Starting involves holding the edge of the board flat in the water, bringing the knees to the chest and extending the arms. Once you are up out of the water and on your feet it's relatively easy to control the board.

After both of us had mastered the sidebar we moved onto the towrope. As our first few attempts resulted in swallowing several mouth-fuls of lakewater, Gavin intervened with some much-needed teaching points. We were soon up out of the water and gliding behind the boat. As with many freestyle sports such as snow-boarding and surfing, there is an endless array of tricks. Tricks are performed on the surface of the water as well as in the air. Wakeboarding tricks include grabs, spins, surface tricks and inverts. I tried my hand at a couple of unimpressive wake jumps and several more impressive falls before calling it a day. The fun and excitement in wakeboarding comes from the speed of movement and pulling off tricks. Give it a go – you won't be disappointed.

Getting there:

The Irish Aquatic Sports Centre (IASC) is only twenty minutes from Blanchardstown, Dublin. From Dublin take the N3 as far as the Fairyhouse cross, taking the left turn for Trim/Batterstown. Drive for another 10 km, passing through Batterstown. Once past the Warrenstown Arms pub take the first left turn for Summerhill. Drive for another 4 km and you should see the black gates and a sign for the IASC on the left, directly before the small crossroads with Dorey's Forge pub on the right.

The area:

The IASC is located on a privately owned manmade lake in Summerhill, Co. Meath.

Provider:

The Irish Aquatic Sports Centre (IASC) has two speed boats, a banana boat, inflatable tubes, a range of wetsuits and changing rooms with showers. You will need to bring a bathing suit and towel.

One lesson will cost you €40, two lessons for €70, three for €90 and four for €120. If you'd like to become a club member, annual membership will cost you €350 per person per year with each subsequent lesson costing €15. (IASC: Gavin +353 (0)86 601 6340;

Éamonn +353 (0)86 836 6410, www.wakeboardingwaterskiing.com)

More about Wakeboarding:

Wakeboarding is said to be the fastest growing water sport in the world. If you can water ski or snowboard you will most likely pick up wakeboarding quite quickly. If you are interested in learning, contact one of the many centres around the country.

For a comprehensive list of Wakeboarding/Waterskiing clubs and centres around Ireland check out the club listing on the Irish waterski federation website (www.iwsf.ie).

Accommodation:

Summerhill is only twenty minutes from Dublin. For accommodation options in Dublin see www.visitdublin.com or contact the Dublin tourist office from within Ireland at (1850 230 330) or from outside Ireland at (+353 (0)66 979 2083).

For accommodation options in the Meath area contact the Trim tourist office at +353 (0)46 943 7227 (open Mon–Sat 9.30 a.m. to 5.30 p.m, Sunday and bank holidays 12 noon to 5.30 p.m.) or see www.meathtourisim.ie.

Other attractions:

There are plenty of interesting heritage sites in Meath; the hill of Tara and Brú na Bóinne are two worth visiting. Spectacular views can be had from the top of the hill of Tara, the ancient inauguration site of the high kings of Ireland. Brú na Bóinne is one of the world's most important archaeological landscapes, which includes the passage tombs of Newgrange, Knowth and Dowth.

Other activities worth trying in the area are fishing, air ballooning and horse riding –the Boyne valley area is renowned for fantastic wild brown trout fishing (see www.fishingireland.net for further information about permits). Fairyhouse racecourse, the home of the Irish Grand National, holds regular horse racing meetings. Irish Balloon rides in Trim take up to four people in one of their balloons over the Meath area (www.balloons.ie).

Best time to go/season:
The centre is open all year round, but for enjoyable water temperatures try any time between May and September.

Links:
www.wakeboardingwaterskiing.com;
www.thewwa.com;
Irish Waterski Federation: www.iwsf.ie.

CYCLING SLIEVE BLOOM MOUNTAINS, CO. LAOIS

Once the childhood home of the mythical Irish warrior, Fionn MacCumhaill, the Slieve Bloom mountains are surrounded by flat land, dark green forests, deep valleys, waterfalls, rivers and bogs. While they rise to only 539 metres at Árd Éirinn, they manage to visually dominate the southern midlands of Ireland.

The day didn't exactly start out to plan; after a failed puncture repair I ended up changing bikes before leaving Portlaoise. As we left Portlaoise travelling northeast on the Ballyfin road we discovered that, although the narrow road had few cars travelling on it, they all seemed intent on driving our bikes into a ditch. The omens were bad. Before entering the town of Ballyfin we took a right detour towards Ballyfin House. The magnificent house is located on a large woodland park that in-

cludes a 30-acre man-made lake. The Patrician Brothers ran a secondary school there from 1928 to 2003. Now under private ownership, the house is currently being restored and will soon open its doors as a hotel. The way our day was going we were disappointed, but not surprised, to find the gates to the grounds closed. I have fond memories of visiting the house as a child and being fascinated by the 'round room' and transfixed by the menagerie of stuffed animals that adorned the walls and halls of the house.

We decided to press on and see if our luck would turn. We took a short detour to view the Cathole Falls, a small natural pool of water and popular picnic area along the Owenass river. I vividly remember regularly swimming here as a child and the exhilaration of leaping into the black pool from the highest rock – and the rain of verbal abuse showered upon those who wouldn't jump. Nothing prepares you for the disappointment you feel as an adult when you return to the site of your former glories only to discover that your memory has grossly exaggerated reality. The pool of mountain water looked considerably smaller and felt significantly colder than I had remembered. We cycled on, my mind turning over other potentially flawed memories. After another short climb we descended quickly into the small village of Rosenallis, where we turned left for Clonaslee village and the most challenging part of the cycle – 'the Cut' mountain pass.

A thigh-burning 4 km-steep climb took us to the top of the mountain pass. From here we had a clear view over the extensive blanket

bog landscape. Exhausted upon reaching the top, we took a much needed food break at the viewing point. We hadn't sat down for five minutes when we heard thunder in the distance and large black clouds started to close in around us. Apparently it rains 325 days of the year in the Slieve Bloom mountains. Wasting no time we hit the road, on a white-knuckle ride down a steep winding mountain road, to an unexpected right-hand hairpin bend. It was here my guide tried to convince me that just after the bend you can experience 'anti-gravity'. If you park your car on the hill, the car will appear to roll uphill, apparently caused by a natural illusion, a result of the unusual lie of the land in the area. We couldn't test the theory since at this stage the lightning was very close and the rain extremely heavy. At

Burke's crossroads we took a left turn and followed the long flat road in torrential rain back through Ballyfin and into Portlaoise.

The Slieve Bloom mountains offer challenging rides through small country villages along quiet country roads. The mountains are one of the few scenic spots of unspoiled countryside in Ireland. They are not yet overrun with tourists, so make the most of it while it lasts.

Getting there:

Portlaoise, the starting and finishing point of the cycle, is located in the heart of the midlands on the main Cork to Dublin motorway. By road take the N7 from Dublin or Limerick or the N8 from Cork. Portlaoise railway station operates daily services to Dublin, Cork, Limerick and

Tralee (www.irishrail.ie). Bus Éireann (www.buseireann.ie) has many bus services serving Portlaoise from all major towns and cities.

The area:

The Slieve Bloom mountains are located in central Ireland. Despite their accessibility, the mountains and villages generally attract small numbers of tourists. Much of the higher reaches of the mountains have been designated as an environmentally protected area for special preservation. As a result there are plenty of signposted walks, designated picnic areas and information boards on flora and fauna. Árd Éirinn (meaning height of Ireland) is the highest point, stretching to 529 metres; on a clear day it is said you can see fifteen counties. The mountaintop is one of the few remaining intact blanket bog landscapes. Blanket bog is formed in areas of high rainfall where the rain washes surface minerals from the soil, depositing these minerals lower down where they form impermeable layers known as iron pan. The water cannot soak through this layer, resulting in a waterlogged soil surface and the formation of peat.

Provider:

Bikes can be hired at M Kavanagh, Railway Street, Portlaoise (+353 (0)57 8621357). Rental from June to September.

More about Cycling:

The route is a total of 71 km and takes between 2.5 and 4.5 hours. Apart from the stretch of road between Portlaoise and Ballyfin the majority of this cycle is on quiet country roads. The long climb from Clonaslee to the top of 'the Cut' is demanding, and the winding ride down the other side requires constant concentration. If you're out for a more challenging ride, add the climb to the top of the Glendine gap (410 metres); follow the signposts from Drimmo. The Slieve Bloom mountains are notorious for bad weather, so check the forecast before you set out and make sure to carry wet-weather gear. There are plenty of small towns along the route where you can stop and take a break. For a comprehensive list of cycling clubs in Ireland check out the club directory on www.cyclingireland.ie

Accommodation:

B&Bs in the Portlaoise area include Dermot O'Sullivan's B&B (+353 (0)57 862 2774, town centre), Oakville B&B (+353 (0)57 866 1970, Mountrath Rd), Laois County Lodge (+353 (0)57 862 0472, Dublin Rd) and Ivyleigh House (+353 (0)57 862 2081, near railway station). Hotels: Heritage hotel (+353 (0)57 867 8588, www.theheritagehotel.com), O'Loughlins hotel (+353 (0)57 862 1305, Main Street) and The Comfort Inn (+353 (0)57 869 5901, www.choicehotels.ie). Alternatively, overnight in one of the small friendly villages on the route. For a complete list of accommodation options see the accommodation section on www.discoverireland.ie.

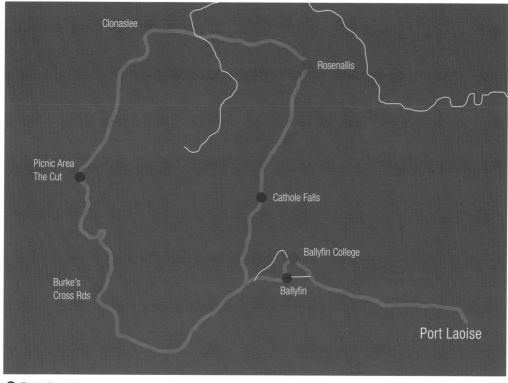

● Tourist Attraction
● Town

Other attractions:

Slieve Bloom mountains are the main attraction of the area. There are numerous walking routes through the mountains, for example the Slieve Bloom Way, a 77km circular walking trail that passes remarkable deep glens, rock outcrops, waterfalls and lofty summits (www.walkireland.ie). Just outside Portlaoise lies the Rock of Dunamaise, an ancient Celtic fortification that can be seen from the Portlaoise by-pass. The impressive view from the top is well worth the climb. Other activities in the area include sky diving in Clonbullogue, Co. Offaly (1850 260 600, www.skydive.ie), fishing on the upper Barrow and Nore rivers, horse riding at Kinnitty Castle Equestrian Cen-

tre (www.kinnittycastle.com) and horse-drawn caravan hire in Coolrain village (+353 (0)57 873 5178, www.horsedrawncaravans.com).

Best time to go/season:

May to September is, in general, the driest period. The heather at the end of the summer displays vibrant colours which are not to be missed.

Links:

www.slievebloom.ie;
www.cyclingireland.ie;
www.rosenallis.com;
www.clonaslee.net;
www.ballyfin.com.

CANOEING
RIVER BARROW,
ST. MULLINS, CO. CARLOW

Having strapped a large Canadian canoe to the roof rack we packed the car with buoyancy aids, paddles, a picnic and some fishing rods. All we were short of was the fishing bait. We stopped in the scenic village of Graiguenamanagh in search of bait and were quickly directed to Boyles pub and hardware shop. We waited while a local ordered a pint of Guinness – it was worth the wait. We left with a fishing spinner and directions to St Mullins.

St Mullins is a small riverside town nestled between the Backstairs mountains and Brandon hill; it was also the spot recommended for launching our canoe. The mooring canal was located down a riverside road which was more pothole than road. The canal at St Mullins is the last place hired boats can navigate down the Barrow navigation waterway, which runs for 65 km from Athy in Co. Kildare to St Mullins in Co. Carlow. Lateral canals bypass shallow sections along the river.

Planning on a leisurely fishing trip on the Barrow, we opted for the open/Canadian canoe. The canoe, which originated with the native tribes of North America, was used to transport people and goods across the large expansive lakes of Canada. Its larger open design has plenty of storage space and is usually manned by two people using a paddle with one blade, as opposed to the closed kayak, which is generally manned by one person with a two-bladed paddle.

With the canoe packed and buoyancy aids on, we set off upriver to where the short canal joins the fast-flowing river. It had been a particularly wet summer and the water level was quite high. Indeed, it took us a bit of time to find our rhythm and steer the canoe in a straight line. We quickly learned, however, that working our way upriver was easier when we kept the canoe in the slower-moving water close to the river bank.

A couple of kilometres upstream we found a spot along the river bank to eat our picnic and cast the fishing lines. We cast out for about an hour before admitting defeat. The Barrow is, apparently, one of the best course fishing rivers in the country with good size bream, perch, pike, rudd, roach, dace and hybrids, as well as an annual run of shad in May. Trout and salmon are fished from March to September. Eels, too, have long been associated with Graiguenamanagh; the monks of Duiske Abbey controlled eel fishing on the river for centuries.

Satisfied that neither of us was going to catch any fish we decided to stick with canoeing. We packed up the gear and headed

another kilometre or so upstream. On reaching a quiet patch we decided to swing the canoe around and ride the current back to St Mullins; it took little time and effort to reach the entrance to the side canal. A large skull and crossbones sign is a clear indicator to boats that crossing the shallow weir is not advisable.

The river Barrow offers opportunities for both budding whitewater canoeists to try their hand at crossing the low-grade rapids formed by the many weirs along the river and day trip canoeists interested in leisurely exploring the tranquil Barrow waterway. Either way I can highly recommend getting out there and paddling your own canoe.

Getting there:

St Mullins is in south Co. Carlow, approximately 126 km south of Dublin, 44 km south of Carlow town, 13 km north of New Ross and 155 km northeast of Cork. From Carlow town follow the signs for Bagenalstown. Drive straight through Bagenalstown to Borris village, then through Borris on the R729 towards New Ross. At Glynn village take a right turn for St Mullins. From Kilkenny city follow the signs for Gowran and then Graiguenamanagh, cross the bridge in Graiguenamanagh and take a right turn onto the St Mullins road. St Mullins is not easy to access by public transport. Irish rail will take you as far as Thomastown in Co. Kilkenny (www.irishrail.ie). Bus Éireann run buses to New Ross, Carlow and Kilkenny (www.buseireann.ie).

The area:

The Barrow is Ireland's second longest river. It rises in the Slieve Bloom mountains in Laois and runs almost 200 km to the sea in waterford.

The river flows south through Mountmellick, Portarlington, Monasterevan, Carlow and new Ross. Between the towns and villages, the Barrow passes through some of the most beautiful woods, valleys and countryside.

The Barrow can be canoed as far north as Mountmellick, but the upper reaches are shallow and obstructed by flood debris. Portarlington is a better starting point. The navigation south of St Mullins is tidal and joins the sea south of New Ross.

See www.waterwaysireland.org for more information about the Barrow navigation including a detailed map of the Barrow navigation.

Provider:

The Flow River Adventures offers guided river trips and canoe hire on both the river Barrow and river Nore (www.gowiththeflow.ie, +353 (0)87 252 9700). Dunmore East Adventure Centre offers whitewater kayak and canoe trips on the river Barrow (www.dunmoreadventure.com, +353 (0)51 383 783).

More about Canoeing:

Ireland, North and South, has a lot to offer the recreational paddler, from the wide open lakes of Lough Erne, Lough Allen, Lough Derg and Lough Ree to the meandering channels of the Lower Bann and the Shannon navigation and the still waters of the Grand and Royal canals, the Barrow navigation and the Shannon–Erne waterway. A way-marked canoe trail is planned for the Barrow navigation.

There are numerous clubs around the country and outdoor centres offering courses and equipment rental. For more information about canoeing in Ireland and a comprehensive list of canoe/kayak clubs; contact the Irish Canoe Union at (+353 (0)1 625 1105) or check out their website www.canoe.ie.

Accommodation:

Local B&Bs include Mulvarra House (www.mulvarra.com, +353 (0)51 424936, St Mullins), Waterside guest house (www.watersideguesthouse.com, +353 (0)59 972 4246), Westend guesthouse (+353 (0)59 972 4868, Graiguenamanagh), Brandon View (www.brandonviewbandb.com, +353(0)59 972 4625, Graiguenamanagh) and Ballyogan House (www.ballyoganhouse.com, +353 (0)59 972 5969, Graiguenamanagh). Expect to pay between €30 and €45 pp for an ensuite room. For a comprehensive list of accommodation options in the area see the accommodation section on www.discoverireland.com.

Other attractions:

There is a diverse range of walking routes available in the area, from gentle riverbank walks to mountain hikes on nearby Brandon hill or the Blackstairs mountains. The Barrow Towpath, the South Leinster Way and the Barrow Way walking trails pass through Graiguenamanagh. The Barrow Towpath was used in the past by horses towing barges laden with barley destined for the breweries and distilleries of Dublin. The South Leinster Way (102 km) and the Barrow Way (113 km) are two long-distance signposted walking trails and part of the national way-marked walking routes (www.walkireland.ie). Mount Leinster is a popular paragliding and hang gliding location (see chapter: Paragliding – Mount Leinster, Co. Wexford).

The Barrow, nearby Brandon lake and the river Nore provide plenty of fishing possibilities. The section between Inistioge and Thomastown provides some of the best locations on the Barrow. Waterways Ireland promotes a catch and release policy on all its waterways. No permits or licences are required for fishing on waterways in the Republic of Ireland that are under the auspices of Waterways Ireland.

The Barrow navigation waterway is becoming a popular destination for barges and cruisers. Barge hire is available from Valley Boats, Barrow Lane, Graiguenamanagh (+ 353 (0)503 24945) The Graiguenamanagh regatta, which takes place on the August bank holiday each year, is reputed to be the oldest regatta on Ireland's inland waterways. Nearby golf courses include Mount Juliet, Borris, Carlow and Enniscorthy. St Mullins was a place of great ecclesiastical importance in the fifth and sixth centuries, and the ruins of small churches and oratories from that time can still be seen. St Mullins was the burial place of Art MacMurrough Kavanagh, one time king of Leinster.

Best time to go/season:

Any fine summer's day. Winter months tend to be the best for whitewater canoeing when water levels are at their highest.

Links:

www.canoe.ie;
www.waterwaysireland.org/barrownav;
www.barrowline.ie (for barrage hire);
www.iwai.ie (Inland Waterways Association of Ireland).

KITESURFING
DOLLYMOUNT STRAND, CO. DUBLIN

It was the last weekend in October, and while most people were out looking for Halloween costumes I was taking my first kiteboarding lesson. I met with François and Catherine, two French ex-pats. They rent a small office in Clontarf, home to the Pure Magic Kiteboarding Centre. Two years ago François, an experienced kiteboarder, was working in Dublin as a mechanical engineer when he stumbled upon Dollymount strand, a shallow open beach located on the outskirts of the city, a perfect kitesurfing beach. When Pure Magic started giving lessons very few people were kiteboarding in Ireland, but interest in the sport is steadily increasing. Pure Magic is now in its second season, offering daily kiteboarding lessons. François and Catherine have never looked back.

Four of us signed up for a three-hour lesson. François took us down to Dollymount beach where he went through the safety aspects of kitesurfing with Seamus and me, both complete beginners. He explained water currents, wind directions, obstacles to be aware of and how to prepare, launch and land the kite safely. Meanwhile the others, having both had lessons before, started preparing their kites. They were hoping to use the board on this outing. It usually takes at least three sessions before you will manage to control the kite enough to even try the board. Snowboarders, surfers and wakeboarders are said to have some advantage when it comes to this stage.

We used the first hour of the session learning to fly the land kite. We tried to con-

trol the kite by flying it in a figure of eight; we then tried to control the landing and launching of the kite. We each took turns practising and quickly got the hang of the basics. François explained that 'the kite is like a tango partner; you have to predict what it will do and make a move to coincide with its movements.' Spoken with a strong French accent gave it an air of authority. Even though the winds were on the low side and we were using the smaller land kite, it still had enough power to pull me off my feet and take me for short runs down the beach. A safety line attached to my right hand allowed me to quickly take the power out of the kite if my feet couldn't keep up or if I took flight.

After comfortably landing and launching the kite a few times, we were ready for the water. We put on our wetsuits, pumped up the larger water kite and made our way to the sea. We started by using the same techniques we used on land to get accustomed to the larger water kite. We then progressed to 'body dragging'. Body dragging is a safe way to practise navigating the kite in the water without the extra threat of injuring yourself with the board. The technique involves bringing the kite above your head, kneeling down in the water and then slowly bringing the kite downwind, causing you to be dragged through the sea. We just managed to get a taster for body dragging before the wind suddenly died down and all the kites hit the water. To really appreciate kitesurfing you have to have the patience to master some of the basic skills initially. You will be rewarded for your perseverance. This sport is pure adrenalin and you won't be disappointed.

Getting there:

Pure Magic is located in front of Dollymount strand at 326 Clontarf Road, Dublin. Dollymount is 3 km north of Dublin city centre and 8 km from Dublin airport. From St Stephen's Green (city centre) drive down Dawson Street and turn right onto Nassau Street. Keep left and follow the road around onto Westland Row and at the bottom of the street, turn left onto Pearse Street.

Continue to the end of Pearse Street, taking a right onto Tara Street. Make sure to stay in one of the right-hand lanes. Drive over Butt Bridge and around by the back of the Customs House and veer left on to Amiens Street. Continue on to Fairview (approx. 2.2 km), passing under the DART bridge at Clontarf. Continue along Clontarf Road until you see the long wooden bridge to Dollymount strand. Pure Magic is located across the road from the bridge.

By public transport take the number 130 bus from Upper Abbey Street; there is a bus stop across the road from the wooden bridge to Dollymount strand.

The area:

Dollymount strand is a long stretch (5 km) of sand in the north side of the city on a man made island – Bull Island. There are two golf clubs on the island and a protected wild bird and seal

€395 for the full package (four sessions), while a private lesson (two hours) costs €150. You will need to call ahead to make a reservation. A deposit of €100 is required to secure a place.

Pure Magic provides all training equipment, trainer kites, four-line and five-line inflatable kites in all sizes from 2m² to 15m², twin-tip boards, lifejackets and helmets. You will need to bring a swim suit, sunglasses, hat and footwear. A wetsuit is optional; if you don't have one you can rent one from Pure Magic.

sanctuary on the northern tip. Bull Island is less than two centuries old, having been formed by a build-up of sand following the construction of the North Bull Wall (designed by Captain William Bligh, of *Mutiny on the Bounty* fame) in the early nineteenth century to maintain a clear channel to Dublin port.

Provider:
Pure Magic (+353 (0)1 487 5157, www. puremagic.com) runs kitesurfing lessons every windy day of the week beginning early March and ending in early December. There are three sessions each day from either Dollymount strand or Sutton beach, depending on the conditions. Lessons with one of its certified kiteboarding instructors costs €135 for one session (half day), €240 for two sessions and

More about Kitesurfing
Kitesurfing is also commonly known as kiteboarding. The sport began in the 1980s but only really gained popularity in the late 1990s. Kitesurfing combines skills from several sports, including kite flying, surfing and wakeboarding.

Kitesurfing involves standing on a board with foot straps/bindings and using a large powerful kite to propel you across the water. The kitesurfer can reach high speeds and perform jumps upwards of 20 feet in height. You can kitesurf on flat water or on waves. Some kitesurfers like wave riding, some like executing big jumps, some like performing tricks and others just like cruising.

Kitesurfing is still relatively new to Ireland, but with a good selection of safe beaches and no shortage of wind the sport is quickly gaining popularity.

If you're interested in taking up the sport, take a lesson with one of the many kitesurfing instructors around the country. Check out the www.kitesurf.ie website for a list of instructors and schools throughout Ireland.

Accommodation:

There is no shortage of accommodation in Dublin city. Check out the accommodation section on www.visitdublin.com or www.discoverireland.ie or contact the Dublin tourist office from within Ireland at (1850 230 330) or from outside Ireland at (+353 (0)66 979 2083).

Other attractions:

In the Clontarf area you can visit:

o Dublin's second largest park, St Anne's park and rose gardens.

o The site of the battle of Clontarf where Brian Boru, the high king of Ireland, in 1014 defeated the invading Vikings. A well on Castle Avenue was later erected to mark the event.

o Visit the Bram Stoker Dracula experience, which features a tour through the story of Dracula and an insight into the author, Bram Stoker, who was born in Clontarf in 1847 (Open 12 noon to 10 p.m. Friday to Sunday, +353 (0)1 805 7824).

o Bull Island provides a nearby amenity for Dubliners who use it regularly for sunbathing, swimming and walking, although you may have to walk a while to reach the water when the tide goes out. There are also two golf clubs on the island, one private and one public.

o Nearby Howth Head (see chapter: Hill Walking – Howth Head, Co. Dublin).

Best time to go/season:

Pure magic offers lessons from March to December.

Links:

www.kitesurf.ie;
www.puremagic.ie.

HILL WALKING
SPINC AND GLENEALO VALLEY ROUTE, GLENDALOUGH, CO. WICKLOW

Glendalough is deservedly one of Ireland's most visited attractions. This fascinating monastic settlement is nestled between two lakes in a beautiful woodland valley. Nine marked walking trails ranging from short (45-minute) walks to longer (four-hour) treks explore the impressive archaeological sites, lakes and mountains of the Glendalough national park.

On advice from the visitor centre I chose to take the Spinc and Glenealo valley route, the most popular walking trail in Glendalough. I set off from the busy information centre towards the nearby St Kevin's monastic site. The site has a magnificent collection of buildings, including the seventh-century cathedral, the round tower (103 feet high) and St Kevin's house (also known as St Kevin's kitchen), which is a double-vaulted oratory.

The route took me through the monastic site, over a wooden bridge and along the right bank of the lower lake. I walked down a long railed wooden boardwalk traversing the marshy land, the tree flanked path eventually opening up to give an impressive view of the lower lake. This path extends all the way up to a second car park beside the upper lake.

At the upper lake I took the old miners' road beside the lake. I spent some time trying to spot St Kevin's bed and Temple-Na-Skellig on the opposite side of the lake. Saint Kevin's bed is a small man-made cave located 10 metres above the lake which is reputed to have been a place of retreat and meditation for St Kevin. The remains of Temple-na-Skellig, a small rectangular stone church, are located nearby at the base of the cliffs. There are plenty of legends surrounding the life of St Kevin, the most famous of which involved a woman who tried to seduce handsome Kevin. Kathleen of the 'eyes of most unholy blue' pursed Kevin despite his holy vows. In a rage Kevin is said to have beat her with a bunch of nettles. She later sought his forgiveness and is said to have become a very holy woman.

At the end of the old miners' road lies the ruins of a miners' village. The area was once rich with minerals such as lead, zinc and silver. This mine ceased operation late in the nineteenth century but the remains of many buildings still stand and the spoil heaps descending from the disused mines are clearly visible. The steep ascent up the mountainside started from the mining village and followed the Glenealo river up to a wooden bridge crossing. I stopped at the bridge to take in the breathtaking view down the valley.

From here I walked across hundreds of railway sleepers covered in chicken wire, laid to protect the mountain heath against the huge numbers of walkers on the mountain every year. The path followed the mountain ridge for a couple of kilometres with spectacular views of the upper and lower lakes, Camaderry mountain and Glenealo valley. The descent passed quickly, winding down through a thick wood beside the Poulanass waterfall and eventually back to the car park below. The Spinc and Glenealo valley takes in dramatic scenery through one of Ireland's most fascinating archaeological sites. A walk not to be missed.

Getting there:

Travelling by car, from the N11 take the exit for Glendalough at Kilmacanogue. Continue on this road, passing through Roundwood and Laragh villages. Just after the sign for the Wicklow Gap, take a left turn into the visitor centre car park.

From the N81, turn off at Hollywood and drive over the scenic Wicklow Gap. On reaching the T-junction at the other side of the mountains, turn right. The visitor car park is the next left.

St Kevin's bus service runs daily departures from Dublin city centre to Glendalough (www.glendaloughbus.com, +353 (0)1 281 8119). Twice daily buses depart from outside the Mansion house on Dawson Street. Phone for the latest timetable. The nearest train station is 13 km from Glendalough at Rathdrum. Take the Dublin–Rosslare train from Connolly station (www.irishrail.ie). You can take a taxi from Rathdrum (Rathdrum Cabs +353 (0)87 956 1111).

The area:

The Gaelic for Glendalough is Gleann Dá Locha, meaning the valley of the two lakes. Ancient glaciers carved out this u-shaped valley, leaving behind majestic granite cliffs, a sheltered woodland valley and the deep waters of the upper and lower lakes. The valley has one of the most important monastic sites in Europe, founded by St Kevin in the sixth century. The site is dominated by a 33-metre high round tower, one of the best preserved in the country, built to protect the monks' priceless manuscripts from Viking raids. Glendalough national park was established in 1991 and is part of the Wicklow mountains national park. It now extends to more than 170 sq km.

More about Hill Walking:

Glendalough has nine marked routes; a detailed map showing all the routes is available from the Glendalough visitor centre. You can read more about them on the www.wicklownationalpark.ie website.

The Spinc route is one of the most enjoyable of all the routes and leads you through

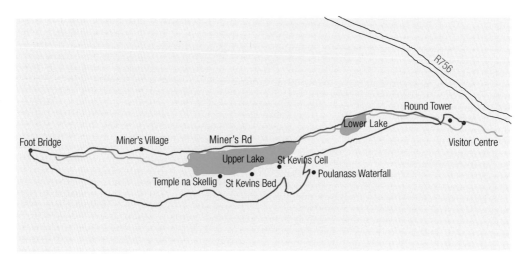

Round Tower
Lower Lake
Visitor Centre
R756
Foot Bridge
Miner's Village
Miner's Rd
Upper Lake
St Kevins Cell
Temple na Skellig
St Kevins Bed
Poulanass Waterfall

● Tourist Attraction

some of the most spectacular scenery in Co. Wicklow. The name comes from the Gaelic 'an spinc' which means 'pointed hill'. This moderate 9-km walk begins and finishes at the Glendalough visitor centre and takes between three and four hours to complete. The route climbs to a height of 380 metres along well maintained paths and railway sleepers. The highest part of the walk is along the mountain ridge, giving spectacular views of the Glenealo valley (home to a large herd of deer) and the two Glendalough lakes. The route is well signposted and easy to follow.

For more information about hill walking in Ireland and a comprehensive list of hill walking clubs; contact the Mountaineering Council of Ireland at (+353 (0)1 625 1115) or check out their website www.mountaineering.ie.

Accommodation:

The Glendalough hostel (www.anoige.ie, +353 (0)404 45342) is the closest, located near the upper lake. There are two other hostels located

13 km away in Rathdrum: Cedar Lodge hostel, Rathdrum (+353 (0)1 830 4555) and the Old Presbytery hostel (+353 (0)404 46930). Glendalough hotel is located within the valley (www.glendaloughhotel.com, +353 (0)404 45135), while Lynhams (www.lynhamsoflaragh.ie, +353 (0) 404 45514) and Derrybawn house hotel (www.derrybawnhouse.com, +353 (0) 404 45073) are located in nearby Laragh. There are numerous B&Bs in the area, including Tudor Lodge (www.tudorlodgeireland.com, + 353 (0)404 45554) and Riversdale House (www.glendalough.eu.com, +353 (0)404 45858). For self-catering accommodation try Glenmalure Lodge (+353 (0)87 231 1656), located in the grounds of the Glenmalure golf club.

For more accommodation options see the accommodation section on the www.visit-wicklow.ie website.

Other attractions:

The Wicklow national park provides an abundance of outdoor activities. The Glenadalough granite cliffs are a popular rock-climbing location with climbs varying from between one and four pitches up to 100 metres in length. There are plenty of walking routes in the area; experienced walkers may want to try the Wicklow way (www.wicklowway.com), a 132-km trail beginning on the outskirts of Dublin city, St Kevin's way (30 km), following in the footsteps of St Kevin through the hills of Co. Wicklow or climb nearby Lugnaquilla mountain, the highest mountain in Wicklow. For a more leisurely challenge try walks through Glenmalure valley or around Lough Dan. For a list of walking routes in the area see www.wicklow.ie or www.walkireland.ie. Adventure Agency (www.adventure.ie), Kippure Corporate (www.kippure.com) and Ireland Extreme (www.irelandxtreme.ie) offer a range of outdoor adventure activities in the Wicklow area, while nearby Clara Lara fun park provides action-packed activities for families and groups of children (www.claralara.com, +353 (0)404 46161).

Best time to go/season:
Good all year round.

Links:
www.discoverireland.com
www.npws.ie (National Parks and Wildlife Service);
www.wicklownationalpark.ie;
www.walking.ireland.ie
www.wicklow.com/glendalough,
www.visitwicklow.ie.

HILL WALKING

CO. DUBLIN

The rain had just stopped and the sun was starting to break through the cloud cover when two of my friends and I set off from Howth harbour. It was surprising to learn that, despite having spent many years in Dublin, none of us had ever walked Howth head before. Although still a bustling fishing port, the harbour was mainly filled with private yachts and speedboats. On the hillside above the east pier stands a commanding Martello tower with its 2.5-m thick walls. It is one of a series of thirty-four towers dotted along the coastline which were built by the British in the early nineteenth century to protect Ireland from a feared Napoleonic invasion.

At the end of Harbour Road we continued around the peninsula and onto Balscadden Road, veering left onto Kolrock Road. The first part of the walk took us through suburban streets until we turned left onto Upper Cliff Road and then a muddy path through the co-conut-scented blooming heath. From here we got our first clear view north to Lambay island and Ireland's Eye, with Dublin city and the Wicklow mountains to the south. At the highest point of the walk (171 metres) we stopped to take in the impressive views. On a clear day the peak of Slieve Donard in the Mourne mountains can be seen, all of 90 km away.

By this point the weather had picked up considerably; the sun was shining and the jackets were off. We walked down the narrow path to the Baily lighthouse, taking in the colourful view to our left of the flower-cloaked cliffs. Disappointingly, there was no access allowed past the lighthouse walls down to the lighthouse tower. The Baily lighthouse was the last of Ireland's eighty-two lighthouses to become fully automated. First erected in 1667, the tower said goodbye to its light keepers in 1997 and now houses radar and communication equipment.

We took our time returning along the

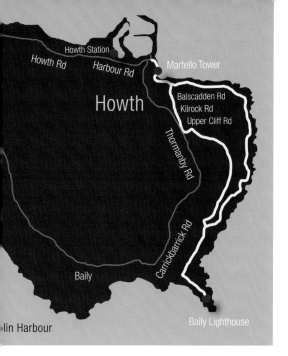

Howth Station
Howth Rd
Harbour Rd
Martello Tower
Howth
Balscadden Rd
Kilrock Rd
Upper Cliff Rd
Thormanby Rd
Carrickbarrick Rd
Baily
lin Harbour
Baily Lighthouse

The area:

Once a small fishing village that featured in James Joyce's *Ulysses*, Howth is now an affluent busy suburb of Dublin. Fresh, locally caught fish can be bought in the village or sampled at one of the many restaurants. The heath lands and coastline of the Howth peninsula are a popular and easily accessible area for Dubliners escaping city life. In 1999 Fingal County Council recognised the importance of the area by designating a large part of it as a special amenity area. Although most of the land of the peninsula is in private ownership, a 21-km extensive network of public rights of way takes you to every large area of heathland and woodland.

More about Hill Walking:

The 'coastal path route' is an easy walk that takes you along laneways and well-worn clifftop paths. Bring comfortable shoes or walking boots, rain gear, warm clothes and water. The route is approximately 6 km and will take between two and three hours.

Exercise caution when walking along the exposed cliff path.

There are four mapped walking routes at Howth head, namely the coastal path route, the bog of frogs loop, the tramline loop and the masts loop. All are only a slight deviation from each other. A map of the different loops is available on the www.discoverireland.ie website.

For a much longer route start at Howth harbour and follow the cliff path to the Baily lighthouse. At the lighthouse continue along the coastal path until you reach the Marine hotel

narrow cliff edge path back to the harbour. In places the winding path was enclosed in heather up to our waist while in others the path hugged the exposed cliff edge. It took no time at all before we were back in Howth village ordering fish and chips from the popular Beshoff's fish and chip shop.

Getting there:

Howth village is a coastal village located 15 km northeast of Dublin city centre and 12 km from Dublin airport. Howth is easily accessible by both train and bus. Take the northbound DART rail service for twenty minutes from the city centre (Pearse Street or Tara Street stations) to Howth DART station. Trains leave every fifteen minutes from the city centre. Dublin Bus number 31 will take you to Howth harbour and the 31B up to Howth's summit. Both busses leave from Eden Quay, located just off O'Connell Street. The walk begins from the end of Howth harbour.

in Sutton. From Sutton you can catch a bus or DART to the city centre or, optionally, complete the loop and walk back to Howth village.

For more information about hill walking in Ireland and a comprehensive list of hill walking clubs; contact the Mountaineering Council of Ireland at (+353 (0)1 625 1115) or check out their website www.mountaineering.ie.

Accommodation:

Howth is only twenty minutes by DART from the centre of Dublin. If you want to stay in Howth village you can try either the Deer Park hotel (www.deerpark-hotel.ie, +353 (0)1 832 2624 or the Bailey Court hotel (www.baily-hotel.com, + 353 (0)1 832 2691,) or stay at one of the many B&Bs: these include Gleann na Smol (+353 (0)1 832 2936), Inisradharc (+353 (0)1 832 2306) and Hazelwood (www.hazelwood.net, +353 (0)1 839 1391). For a comprehensive list of accommodation options in Dublin check the www.visitdublin.com website or contact the Dublin tourist office from within Ireland at 1850 230 330 or from outside Ireland at +353 (0)66 979 2083.

Other attractions:

Howth is a bustling village that offers visitors a myriad of attractions, including Lambay Island, Ireland's Eye, Howth castle, the National Transport Museum, the Martello tower and the Baily lighthouse. Howth is also a popular area for bird watching, sailing and fishing. The small transport museum has over 100 items of Irish vehicular history on display (www.nationaltrans-

portmuseum.org, + 353 (01) 848 0831, From Sept-May its only open on Saturdays, Sundays and Bank Holidays from 2-5pm, from June-August its open Mon-Sat from 10am-5pm).

Ireland's Eye Island is a bird sanctuary which boasts guillemots, razorbills, fulmars, gulls and gannets. Ferries to Ireland's Eye leave from the harbour when there are enough passengers (€15 adult, €10 child). They can be booked in advance from Island Ferries (www.islandferries.net, + 353 (0)86 845 9154, daily departures between April and October). The castle, which has been owned by the St Lawrence family for eight centuries, is closed to the public, but the grounds are worth exploring. Nearby Dollymount strand is a popular kitesurfing location (see chapter: Kitesurfing – Dollymount Strand, Co. Dublin).

Best time to go/season:

All year round. The walking routes can become congested during the summer months.

Links:

www.discoverireland.ie;
www.visitdublin.com;
www.dublinpass.ie (discounts on more than thirty of Dublin's attractions);
www.walking.ireland.ie;
www.howthismagic.com;
www.walkireland.ie.

COASTSTEERING
HOOK HEAD, CO. WEXFORD

Coasteering involves exploring the coast by climbing, swimming, jumping, crawling and diving along the coastline. People have been doing this for years but only recently has coasteering been offered as an adventure activity at centres around Ireland.

Hook head has been a regular Sunday swimming, snorkelling and, at one point, diving destination for my family since I was a child. In bad weather Hook head can be spectacular; as the waves hit the rugged coastline huge spray shoots up onto the mainland around the lighthouse. In good weather the rocks, cliffs, caves and gullies offer great opportunities for snorkelling and

The conditions were perfect on that summer day – the tide was out, the sky was blue and the sea flat calm. The car park at the lighthouse was full, the majority of people opting to take the coastal walking path or hang out in the lighthouse café. Very few people swim at Hook head as the swell can be quite strong and the rocks covered in skin-ripping barnacles. With wetsuits, booties and a good knowledge of these waters we were well prepared.

We started by jumping in from the lower rocks directly below the lighthouse. The tide was out, giving us a chance to explore a long cave. We swam through the gully and looked down

cavity about 8 metres long. A beam of light shone down from an opening above us, filling the cave with a magical glowing green light. On stormy days water is channelled down the cave and forced up through this 'puffing hole' in the cave roof, shooting a high spray over the rocks in a similar fashion to the blowhole of a whale.

We spent the afternoon climbing along the coastline, jumping and diving in places. A bit of local knowledge helped us choose the safe places to jump. The jumping heights increased steadily as the day went on, the last one reaching a scary 8 metres above the water. Coasteering is an exciting, energetic, sometimes scary adrenalin-fuelled activity, experienced in dramatic land and seascapes. Prepare to become an addict.

Getting there:

Hook head is located on the south coast of Co. Wexford, approximately 139 km from Dublin, 152 km from Cork and 179 km from Shannon. Rosslare ferry port is a 40-minute drive from Hook and offers direct ferries from Rosslare to Britain and France (Irish Ferries: www.irishferries.com; Stena Sealink: www.stenaline.co.uk). Bus Éireann (www.buseireann.ie, +353 (0)51 879000) operates a scheduled bus service to New Ross, Wexford and Rosslare. Irish Rail (www.irishrail.ie) runs services from Rosslare, Limerick and Dublin to Waterford, which is just 25 kilometers away. It also runs daily services from Dublin to Wexford and Rosslare. By car from Rosslare/

Wexford take the R733 to Duncannon Road roundabout, turn left at the roundabout, signposted for Wellington Bridge, then follow the signs for Fethard-on-Sea. From New Ross take the R734 to Fethard-on-Sea.

The area:

Hook head is best known for having one of the world's oldest lighthouses, built in the thirteenth century. The lighthouse is now open to the public, offering magnificent views from the tower. The Saltee Islands lie to the east, and Brownstown head to the west. In the distance the peaks of the Comeragh and Blackstairs mountains can be seen. On the rocks around the head, 250-million-year-old limestone fossils are clearly visible. The waters around Hook are notoriously dangerous, particularly at the entrance to the river estuary; several ship wrecks can be found in the area. On stormy days impressive 30-foot waves are known to crash high against the lighthouse walls.

The phrase 'by hook or by crook' is said to have originated in the seventeenth century from the geography of the area. It's claimed that the phrase is derived from Oliver Cromwell's attempts to take Waterford by Hook (on the east side of the harbour) or by Crook (a village on the west side of the harbour). In October 2007 a significant quantity of oil was discovered off the coast of Hook head.

Provider:

Shielbaggan Outdoor Education Centre (www.oec.ie/shielbaggan, +353 (0)51 389550) has experienced guides who will choose the best coasteering location based on ability and conditions. You will need to bring an old pair of runners, a towel and a pair of togs. The centre will provide you with a helmet, wetsuit and buoyancy aid.

More about Coaststeering

The term 'coasteering' was said to have originated in 1973 from a book called *Sea Cliff Climbing* but only became a popular recreational activity in the 1990s after a guide company in Wales began offering coasteering trips along the Welsh coastline. Coasteering involves climbing, swimming, cliff jumping, cave exploring and diving your way along the coastline. Coasteering is different to sea-level traversing, which usually involves traversing a rock face close to the sea using ropes and climbing harnesses with the aim to stay dry.

Ask locally about sea conditions and safe entry and exit points before going coasteering.

Coasteering activity providers in Ireland:

Kilfinane OEC,Outdoor
Education Centre,Kilfinane,OEC, Kilfinane, Co. Limerick
Phone: + 353 (0)63 91161/91059
Email: info@kilfinaneoec.com
Web: www.kilfinaneoec.com

Gartan OEC

Outdoor Education Centre
Church Hill, Letterkenny, Donegal
Phone: +353(0)749137032
Email: office@gartan.com
Web: www.gartan.com

Achill OEC

Outdoor EducationCentre
Cashel, Bunacurry, Achill, Co. Mayo
Phone: + 353 (0)98 47304 / 47253
Email: achill@oec.ie
Web: www.oec.ie/achill/

Burren OEC

Outdoor EducationCentre
Turlough,Bell Harbour, Clare
Phone: +353 (0)65 778066
Email: burroec@eircom.net
Web: www.burrenoec.com

Cappanalea OEC

Outdoor EducationCentre
Oulagh West
Caragh Lake, Co. Kerry
Phone: +353 (0)66 9769244
Web: www.cappanalea.ie

Shielbaggan OEC

Outdoor Education Centre
The Hook, New Ross,Co.Wexford.
Phone: +353 (0)51 389550
Email: shielbaggan@tinet.ie
Web: www.oec.ie/shielbaggan

Action Outdoors

Activity Centre
53AMagheralone Road,
Ballynahinch, Co Down BT24 8SW
Phone: +44(0)7789 754 565
Email: info@actionoutdoors.info
Web: www.actionoutdoors.info

Activities Ireland

Activity Centre
187 Lower Braniel Road,
Belfast, Co Down BT5 7NP
Phone: +44(0)7971 087 480
Email: info@activitiesireland.co.uk
Web: www.activitiesireland.co.uk

Ardclinis Outdoor Adventure

Activity Centre
11 High Street, Cushendall,Co Antrim BT44 0NB
Phone: +44(0)28 2177 1340
Email: info@ardclinis.com
Web: www.ardclinis.com

Bluelough Castlewellan Forest Park

Activity Centre
Bluelough Castlewellan Forest Park,
Castlewellan, Co Down BT31 9DQ
Phone: +44(0)28 4377 0714
Email:customerservices@mountainandwater.com
Web: www.mountainandwater.com

Mobile Team Adventure

Activity Provider
29 Ashgrove, Newtownards,
Co Down BT23 4HA
Phone: +44(0)28 9180 0809
Email:mobileteamadventure@yahoo.co.uk
Web: www.mobileteamadve

Peak Discovery

Activity Centre
98 Bryansford Road,
Newcastle, Co Down BT33 0LF
Phone: +44(0)28 4372 3933
Email: Dublin@pd-group.eu
Web: www.pd-group.eu

The Outdoor Fox

Activity Centre
268 Ballywalter Road,
Millisle, Co Down BT22 2LZ
Phone: +44(0)7779 295 299
Email: john@theoutdoorfox.com
Web: www.theoutdoorfox.com

TollymoreMountain Centre

Activity Centre
Bryansford, Newcastle,Co Down BT33 0PT
Phone: +44(0)28 4372 2158
Email: admin@tollymore.com
Web: www.tollymore.com

Xplore Outdoors

Activity Centre
15 Glenara Woods, Coleraine,
Co Londonderry BT51 3TR
Phone: +44(0)7734 365 321
Email: xploreoutdoors@hotmail.co.uk
Web: www.xploreoutdoors.co.uk

Accommodation:

Nearby hotels include hotel Naomh Seosamh (+353 (0)51 397129, Fethard-on-Sea) and Dunbrody Country House (+353 (0)51 389600, Arthurstown, New Ross). The nearest camping park is 11 km away (Fethard-on-Sea Caravan & Camping Park, +353 (0)51 397123/397230). There are also plenty of places close to the lighthouse to pitch a tent. Local B&Bs include Herrylock B&B (+353 (0)51 397029), offering double ensuite rooms from €35 to €40 pps, and Grove Farmhouse (+353 (0)51 562304), close to Tintern Abbey. For more accommodation options try the hook tourist office (www.thehook-wexford.com, +353 (0)51 397502).

Other attractions:

Historical sites in the area include Tintern Abbey, located in a picturesque woodland (tours daily July and August, +353 (0)51 562650), Dunbrody Abbey and maze, one of the most vivid and imposing old Cistercian remains in Ireland (open daily April to Sept, +353 (0)51 388603), Duncanon fort, built in 1558 in the expectation of an attack on the area by the Spanish Armada (open daily June to Aug, +353 (0)51 389454), the Kennedy homestead, birthplace of President John F. Kennedy's great-grandfather, Patrick Kennedy (+353 (0)51 388264, www.kennedyhomestead.com) and Loftus Hall, home of the famous eighteenth-century ghost story. The story goes that a stranger came to the door one stormy night and was invited to stay. After a few drinks he took part in a game of cards, and during the game a card fell upon the floor. A lady who bent down to retrieve the card was shocked to discover that the stranger had a cloven foot. As she screamed in terror, the stranger went up in a ball of flames and vanished through the ceiling in a puff of smoke. The house is not open to the public.

Other activities in the area include swimming at one of the many beaches on the peninsula, sea angling, whale watching and a boat ride around the Saltee islands. Boats leave from nearby Kilmore quay (daily trips from the harbour depending on the numbers, July and August).

Best time to go/season:

Coasteering is an all-year-round sport provided you have the right equipment to keep you warm in the winter.

Links:

www.coasteering.org;
www.britishcoasteeringfederation.co.uk.

SEA KAYAKING CASTLE ISLAND, CO. CORK

We prepared our three touring kayaks for an overnight sea kayaking and camping trip. The kayaks have enough storage space for a tent, sleeping bags, a disposable barbecue, food and enough warm clothes to get us through the night. It was only my second time kayaking and first time kayaking on the open ocean. Luckily the conditions were perfect, the sea was flat, the sun shining and there was little wind.

'It doesn't get much better than this,' says my guide.

From the shore we could see the island, roughly 1 km from Schull harbour. There wasn't another person in sight as we kayaked

the short distance from Schull harbour to the island's pier situated just below the castle ruins. The island was ours for the night, well … us and about 30 sheep. We unpacked the kayaks and setup camp.

By 11.00 p.m. the setting sun had cast a beautiful red glow across the sky. We jumped into the kayaks and headed towards the horizon. We planned to make it around the island before it got too dark. At the western tip of the island the lights of Schull village illuminated the inlet on our right, and the rosy glow on the Atlantic Ocean filled our view to the left. As we made our way around the island a shoal of mackerel created a boiling effect in the water around us and the ruins of a nearby cottage formed a perfect silhouette against the backdrop of the red sky.

When we returned to the pier we pulled the kayaks in for the night and made our way back to the tent. The barbecue was prepared on an abandoned road sandwiched between two old stone walls which provided shelter from the night breezes. The road, overrun with grass and weeds, provided a perfect dining area and when lit with candles created a perfect backdrop for our evening meal. The Bandon sausages picked up on our journey from Cork were devoured in no time. Our guide pointed out the near full moon on the horizon, a perfect end to a perfect day.

I awoke early the next morning, and decided to explore the island. I headed towards a couple of ruins on the top of the hill. A narrow road, just wide enough to fit a horse and cart, led me to the site of two ruins at the highest point of the island. From here I had a clear view of the entire island across to the neighbouring

islands (Horse Island and Long Island). It was a crystal clear morning. The only sound was the munching of grass from a nearby sheep.

The rest of the morning was spent practicing rescue techniques in the kayak, I probably should have done this lesson first, but I guess it's better late than never. We packed up our things and made sure to leave no trace of our night on the island. The ten minutes it took to reach the mainland went too quickly. This trip will be hard to beat.

Getting there:

Castleisland is located about 1 km off the coast of Schull village in southwest Cork. Schull is 107 km from Cork city. Take the N71 road west out of Cork city and follow the road signs for Bandon, then Clonakilty and Skibbereen through to Ballydehob and into Schull. If you have time, the coastal road from Cork city to Schull is well worth your while. Bus Éireann runs a service from Cork city to Schull. Check www.buseireann.ie for the latest timetable (route 237).

The area:

The island is small and relatively flat with a handful of cottage ruins spread throughout. Narrow overgrown roads (boreens) connect the cottage ruins. Sheep graze on the island, so camping and walking is easy. If you are planning a longer stay, Castleisland can act as a good base for exploring the neighbouring Horse Island and Long Island.

Provider:

Both Schull Watersport Centre (www.schull-watersports.com, +353 (0)28 28554) and

Atlantic Sea Kayaking (www.atlanticseakayak-ing.com, +353 (0)28 21058), based in Skibbereen, offer a range of different kayak tours, from short half-day trips to longer island-exploring trips throughout West Cork.

More about Kayaking:

The easiest landing point on the island is a beach at the pier, located under the castle on the land-facing side of the island. There is no fresh water on the island, so if you are planning on camping you need to bring all supplies with you. The journey from Schull to Castleisland is relatively short, but inexperienced kayakers should be careful when crossing the open ocean, especially in bad weather conditions. For more information about kayaking in Ireland and a comprehensive list of canoe/kayak clubs; contact the Irish Canoe Union at (+353 (0)1 625 1105) or check out their website www.canoe.ie.

Accommodation:

If possible you should try and spend at least one night in a tent on the island; alternatively, Schull has numerous bed and breakfast op-

tions. For a complete accommodation list pick up the free visitors' guide to Schull, available from village businesses, or check out www.corkkerry.ie or www.schull.ie/stay.htm. Schull is quite popular during the summer months so it may be wise to book ahead.

Other attractions:

Ireland's only planetarium is located in Schull, and is open during the summer months. Mizen head signal station, located 34 km from Schull, is worth visiting, as it offers great views along the south and west coasts. Whale watching boats leave from nearby Union Hall (see chapter: Whale Watching – Union Hall, West Cork).

Best time to go/season:

Anytime between May and August.

Links:

www.corkkerry.ie;
www.oileain.org/oileain5.htm;
www.schull.ie/stay.htm;
www.atlanticseakayaking.com.

BODYBOARDING GARRETTSTOWN, CO. CORK

We arrived in Garrettstown on a sunny day in July with a roof rack stacked with surf and bodyboards. We decided to have a bit of fun bodyboarding the little brother of surfing. We drove past the first beach west of Kinsale called White Strand or Garrylucas where there were few waves and even fewer people. Another 200 meters took us to Garrettstown beach where the car park was full of cars and the beach full of families, surfers and sunbathers. The conditions looked good so we wasted no time unpacking the gear.

We pulled on the wetsuits and jumped in the water. I was with a few friends, a couple of whom have never been bodyboarding before.

The great thing about bodyboarding is that you don't need much skill to have fun.

Basic bodyboarding action involves:

o Lie down on the board and paddle out past the crashing waves.
o With your hands on the board, wait for the first wave. When you see it, begin kicking with your feet to get some speed up.
o To move to the left or right of the wave, you will need to have your hands positioned correctly. If you are going to ride to the left of the wave, your right hand should be on the side of the board while your left hand is on the front.
o Next, pull your body up on the board while holding your head high.
o To build up speed you will need to go up and down the face of the wave.
o If you are wearing flippers, hold them out of the water. Drag them if you want to slow down.

After about an hour of catching waves we were forced into an early lunch as the tide had come all the way into the beach wall. We stopped at a picnic area about half way between Kinsale and Clonakilty and had an impromptu road-side BBQ. We drove on looking out for suitable spot to put the boards back in the water. The postcard perfect town of Clonakilty warranted another stop. We spent an hour checking out the local surf shop and walking the narrow streets which were adorned with impressive flower boxes. No trip to Clonakilty would be complete without stopping for a drink in the best-known watering hole in the town - De Barra's bar. Thirst quenched we headed for the beach. Inchydoney is known for its two magnificent blue flag beaches which are thronged during the Summer months. There is a four star hotel and spa over looking the beach which also offers self catering apart-ments. A surf school operates at the beach and offers board and gear hire and lessons. The tide was on the way out and the waves

were quite poor when we reached Inchydoney so we decided to call it a day. This is the beauty of bodyboarding. Just throw the board in the car and if the conditions look good go for it if not, you haven't committed too much time or energy into the preparation. Bodyboarding can be purely fun at the beginner level or advance to more challenging levels with trimming, spinning and big wave boarding. For a fun activity, which requires few skills starting off, try bodyboarding.

Getting there:

From Cork: Garrettstown beach is about forty minutes' drive from Cork city, just outside the town of Kinsale and village of Ballinspittle. From Cork city follow the signs for Cork airport; at the roundabout at the entrance to the airport take the second exit (R600). Proceed for about 20 km through the villages of Riverstick and Belgooly and into Kinsale. Follow the road along the Bandon river road until you reach a large bridge. Cross over the bridge and stay right, heading for the old head of Kinsale / Ballinspittle. From here follow the signs for Garrettstown. You can either travel via the old head or Ballinspittle village.

Public Transport: Cork city is well served by both train and bus. The Bus Éireann number 249 bus travels frequently between Cork bus station and Garrettstown. Contact Bus Éireann (www.buseireann.ie, +353 (0)21 450 8188) for the latest timetable.

From Clonakilty: As you drive out of Clonakilty towards Cork city turn right at the Shannon

Vale factory and head for Timoleague. As you approach Timoleague follow the signs for Ballinspittle village and then on to Garrettstown. The drive takes about twenty-five minutes.

The area:

There are two beaches at Garrettstown, both of which have blue flag status; the most westerly beach is the more popular one with surfers, but the other (White Strand/Garrylucas) can be good when Garrettstown is closed out. Both beaches have toilet facilities, and lifeguards are on duty on Garrettstown beach during the summer months.

Garrettstown does not have any major rip currents; the only hazards are two sets of man-made groins, designed to keep the sand on the beach, particularly in rough weather. These only become dangerous in mid to high tide conditions. Signs on the beach indicate their location.

Provider:

Gtown Surf School (www.surfgtown.com, +353 (0)87 876 8549, +353 (0)21 477 8884) operates from the car park by the beach most of the year. The school offers surfing lessons, and also rents a range of wetsuits, bodyboards and surfboards to suit all levels and ages.

More about Bodyboarding:

For many, bodyboarding, otherwise known as boogie boarding, is their first introduction to wave riding. Bodyboarding is more affordable and easier to master than surfing. The smaller, lighter boards are also easier to manage for young kids who are not quite ready for a full-sized surf board. You can go from riding whitewash to actually riding a wave much faster than with surfing. The more advanced manoeuvres like trimming, spinners and rollos come with practice.

Bodyboarding was invented by Tom Morey in California in the 1970s. The bodyboard is a small, roughly rectangular piece of hydrodynamic foam usually tied to the wrist or ankle with a leash. The bodyboard is predominantly ridden lying down ('prone'), but can also be ridden in a half-standing stance with one knee touching the board, a position known as 'dropknee'. The bodyboard may even be ridden standing up.

Safety:

Talk to the lifeguard about ocean conditions; wear sun cream; only ride waves your swimming ability can handle. If you get tossed in the waves, don't panic – hold your breath until the tumbling stops and swim to shore.

Etiquette:

As with surfing, follow some basic etiquette. Have respect for other surfers, be friendly in the water and give way to surfers closest to the peak of the wave.

For more information about surfing in Ireland and a comprehensive list of surf schools and clubs; check out the Irish Surfing Association website www.isasurf.ie.

Accommodation:

For cheap accommodation you can camp at the Garrettstown House Holiday Park (www. garrettstownhouse.com, +353 (0)21 477 8156) or stay in the Guardwell hostel in Kinsale (www.kinsalehostel.com, +353 (0)21 477 4686). For more accommodation options in the Kinsale area check out www.kinsale.ie/kinsacco.htm or call the Kinsale tourist office on +353 (0)21 477 2234. For accommodation options in County Cork contact the Cork tourism office on +353 (0)21 427 3251.

Other attractions:

There are plenty of tourist attractions in the Kinsale area. Charles fort, built in 1677, is a classic example of a star-shaped fort and boasts panoramic views of Kinsale harbour. The old head of Kinsale is now home to an exclusive golf course, and access to the head is restricted to club members. You can, however, park at the entrance to the golf club car park and get a good view of the old head by venturing either east or west from the golf club entrance.

Nearby Kinsale is a well established base for maritime sports including sailing, diving and sea angling. The Kinsale Outdoor Education Centre (www.kinsaleoutdoors.com) and the Oysterhaven Centre (www.oysterhaven.com) offer courses and equipment rental for many different adventure activities, while nearby Inchydoney beach outside Clonakilty is another popular surfing spot (www.westcork-surfing.com). For information about kayaking in the Kinsale area check out the chapters:

Sea Kayaking – Sandycove, Co. Cork and
Moonlight Sea Kayking – Kinsale, Co. Cork.

Best time to go/season:
Good all year round. The best waves are from
September to May.

Links:
www.surfgtown.com;
www.ibatour.com (international
bodyboarding association);
www.kinsale.ie.

SEA KAYAKING
SANDYCOVE, CO. CORK

A **popular kayaking** and open-water swimming destination in west Cork, Sandycove offers something for both the experienced kayaker and the complete beginner. Sandycove Island, located only a couple of hundred metres from the harbour, forms a natural barrier from the Atlantic ocean. The creek on on the east side of the harbour is sheltered and provides an ideal location for beginners to master the basics of paddling their sea kayak. More experienced kayakers can explore the old abandoned famine village of Courtaparteen or paddle on towards Black head with its isolated coves.

We unloaded the kayaks and took all the gear down the slipway. The tide was out so we set down the boats on the sand and prepared the gear. We adjusted the feet positions on the two sea kayaks, connected the paddle halves and put on our buoyancy aids. There are many different types of kayak – sea kayaks, whitewater kayaks, surf kayaks, racing kayaks and hybrid kayaks – each suited to different water conditions. A sea kayak or touring kayak is designed for paddling on open water (lakes, bays and the ocean). Sea kayaks opt for stability over manoeuvrability, have a covered deck, generally have under-deck storage, can incorporate a spraydeck and are relatively comfortable to sit in over long distances.

We set out from the harbour towards the western tip of the island. On reaching the island we realised that the waves that looked quite small from the shore were actually not that small. We made our way slowly through the waves and around the tip of the island. It was hard to keep the kayak balanced as the waves hit us side on. On the opposite corner of the island a wave finally got the better of me and I capsized. As I hadn't mastered the Eskimo roll I opted for a quick bail out. I resurfaced to find my fellow kayaker laughing his head off. He soon stopped laughing when, while trying to get back into my kayak, I capsized his kayak too. Fortunately the boats had enough buoyancy to allow us to paddle them even when they were full of water. Our limited kayaking experience dictated that we make a stop on the island to empty the boats. I'm told this can be performed easily at sea but we decided not to risk a third capsize.

The rest of the day was spent exploring the caves and crevices of the coastline and the nearby creek. We finished our day kayak surfing the smaller and more manageable waves on the harbour side of the island, learning much-needed rescue techniques and attempting the coveted Eskimo roll. Sea kayaking is an incredible way to see the Irish coastline. As with all adventure activities safety should be paramount, but there are safe, sheltered harbours and bays all around this country that are ideal for beginners. Equally, there are amazing open water paddles for more experienced kayakers to explore. If you want an unimpeded view of the rugged unspoiled beauty of the Irish coast there is no better way than in a sea kayak.

Getting there:

Sandycove is located 5 km west of Kinsale village in Co. Cork. By Car: Kinsale is located 27km from Cork city, 21km from Cork airport and 22km from Cork ferryport (Ringaskiddy). Blarney is 39 km away, Killarney 87 km and Cobh (via harbour ferry) 32 km.

From Cork city follow the signs for Cork airport. At the roundabout at the entrance to the airport take the second exit (R600) and follow this road for about 20 km through the villages of Riverstick and Belgooly and into Kinsale. From Kinsale follow the R600 signposted Clonakilty. Outside Kinsale take the right turn after the bridge, take the next left signposted Sandycove and then an immediate right turn. The slipway is located within the village.

Public Transport: Cork city is well served by both train and bus. The Bus Éireann number 249 bus travels frequently between Cork bus station and Kinsale. Check www.buseireann.ie or call Bus Éireann on +353 (0)21 450 8188 for the latest timetable. From Kinsale you can take a taxi with Kinsale Cabs (www.kinsalecabs.com, +343 (0)21 470 0100, +353 (0)21 477 2642) to Sandycove.

The Area:

Sandycove is a small sheltered harbour in Co. Cork. Sandycove Island lies about 500 metres from the beach. The privately owned island is home to a few sheep and numerous birds and other wildlife.

Provider:

Both H20 Sea Kayaking (www.h2oseakayaking.com, +353 (0)21 477 8884) and the Kinsale Outdoor Education Centre (www.kinsaleoutdoors.com, +353 (0)21 477 2896) offer canoe and kayak courses to all levels in the Kinsale area. All kayaking equipment is provided. You will need to bring swimming togs/shorts, a towel, a pair of trainers/sandals that you don't mind getting wet, a sun hat/sun cream and a water bottle.

More about Kayaking:

Sandycove is an excellent springboard from which you can explore other sections of coastline such as the old abandoned famine village of Courtaparteen or paddle on towards Black head with its isolated coves. The Cork coastline offers many kayaking possibilities: kayak Kinsale harbour (see chapter: Moonlight Sea Kayaking – Kinsale, Co. Cork), around Oysterhaven bay, Kayak up or down the Bandon river or out around the old head of Kinsale. An annual sea kayaking race takes place around Great Island in Cork each year; for more information see www.greatislandkayakrace.com.

For more information about kayaking in Ireland and a comprehensive list of canoe/kayak clubs; contact the Irish Canoe Union at (+353 (0)1 625 1105) or check out their website www.canoe.ie.

Accommodation:

Guardwell hostel in Kinsale (www.kinsalehostel.com, +353 (0)21 477 4686), Dempseys hostel (+353 (0)21 477 2124), Trident hotel (www.

tridenthotel.com, +353 (0)21 477 2301), Actons hotel (www.actonshotelkinsale.com, +353 (0)21 277 2135). For more accommodation options in the Kinsale area check out www.kinsale.ie/kinsacco.htm,or call the Kinsale tourist office on +353 (0)21 477 2234. For accommodation options in the Cork area contact the Cork tourist office on +353 (0)21 427 3251.

Other attractions:

Sandycove Island is popular with open water swimmers; local swimmers regularly swim the 1,600 metres around the island back to the slipway. The annual swimming race, the 'Sandycove Island challenge', attracts international participants and takes place in September – see www.corkmasters.ie for more information. A short cliff walk west of the slipway looks out over the sea towards the old head of Kinsale. The old head is now home to an exclusive golf course and access to the head is restricted to club members. You can, however, park at the entrance to the golf club and get a good view of the old head by venturing either east or west of the entrance. Kinsale is famous for its gourmet food, art and craft shops and range of leisure activities. Two festivals, Kinsale arts week in early July and the Kinsale food festival in October justifiably attract large crowds. There are plenty of tourist attractions in the Kinsale area. Charles fort, built in 1677, is a classic example of a star-shaped fort and boasts panoramic views of Kinsale harbour. Popular activities in the area include sailing, sea angling, surfing (see chapter; Bodyboarding – Garrettstown, Co. Cork) and whale watching. Diverse wildlife can be spotted in the waters around Kinsale, including seals, whales, dolphins, porpoise and an array of sea birds. Check out www.kinsale.ie for a list of activity providers.

Best time to go/season:

May to September.

Links:

www.kinsale.ie,
www.corkkerry.ie,
www.irishislands.info,
www.atlanticseakayaking.com,
www.irishcanoeunion.com,
www.kinsaletimes.com,
www.discoverireland.ie,
www.vertigokitesurfing.com,
www.irishislands.info,
www.greatislandkayakrace.com.

SURFING
CO. SLIGO AND CO. CLARE

The powerful Atlantic ocean has carved out some of Europe's best surf spots along the west coast of Ireland. Unimpeded for thousands of miles, the rolling waves are some of the biggest in Europe. Surfing is booming in Ireland, mainly due to the increased number of surf schools and locals taking up the sport. Beaches can get a little crowded, particularly during the summer, but it's still possible to find quiet, out-of-the-way spots.

On a bright September evening we set off from Dublin on a road trip to some of the most popular surfing spots along the west coast. The first port of call was Easkey in Co. Sligo, the home of the Irish Surfing Association. Easkey is a small attractive village with a couple of shops and pubs. We arrived quite late, parking at a makeshift camping area at the foot of the fifteenth-century remains of Roslee castle. The following morning we awoke to find both the car park and the waves quite crowded. A full car park on a Wednesday morning in September is testament to the popularity of the sport. What makes Easkey so popular are the two reef breaks, the left just by the river mouth (known as 'Easkey left') and the right to the east of the castle (known as 'Easkey right'). The waves in Easkey break over rocks rather than on sand. This makes the waves more attractive to surfers because they are hollowed and faster than beach breaks. Looking down over Easkey left, we admired the surfers riding the waves in as far as the jagged rocks under the ruins of the castle. It wasn't for the faint hearted. We decided that the reef break was a little too advanced for us. We watched the surfers for a while before deciding to try Enniscrone, a seaside town about 13 km west of Easkey.

Enniscrone boasts a long sandy blue flag beach on the shores of Killala bay. This beginner-friendly beach has both a good beach break and a right-hand point break. A point break is a wave that breaks over a rocky point, a beach break over a sandy seabed and a reef break over a coral reef or a rock seabed. The tide was on the way in and there were only a handful of surfers in the water. The waves weren't ideal but suited us. We spent the morning in the water catching the odd wave.

Happy with our first surf of the trip we packed the gear up and drove south towards the busy surf towns of Lahinch and Spanish Point in Co. Clare. We spent the night in Galway before getting up early to drive the scenic coastal road through the unique limestone landscape of the Burren. A couple of stops later we arrived in Lahinch, where the three-kilometer long beach with its variety of breaks caters for novice, intermediate and experienced surfers. Parts of the west coast of Ireland are among the best in Europe for surf novices, with the advantage of the slower rolling Atlantic waves. Lahinch receives ample swells; conditions are at their best when the wind blows in an easterly direction. We arrived to a crowded beach and a flat calm ocean. One of the lifeguards told us the waves should be good around eight in the evening when the tide was due to come in.

We decided to head 13 km further south to the less popular Spanish Point. The name refers to the wrecking of some Spanish Armada ships off the coast in 1588. We parked the van overlooking the long sandy beach; as the waves got bigger so too did the crowds. Although crowded, there was a friendly atmosphere in the water with enough waves for everyone. We spent a couple of hours here catching some good waves. The sun was setting as we got out of the water, giving a beautiful golden glow to the sandy beach. A perfect end to our surfing safari.

Getting there:

Easkey and Enniscrone, Co. Sligo: Enniscrone is located 13 km from Ballina. If driving from Dublin take the N4 to Longford, the N5 to Swinford and then the N26 to Ballina via Foxford. From Ballina take the N59 Sligo road for about three miles before turning left on to the R298 towards Enniscrone. The beach car park is located past the caravan park in the centre of the town. Easkey is a further 13.5 km from Enniscrone along the same road. Park at the foot of Roslee castle. For directions from other Irish cities see enniscroneonline.com.

Lahinch and Spanish Point, Co. Clare. Lahinch is located 276 km from Dublin. Take the N7 to Limerick, the N18 towards Ennis, and then the N85 to Ennistymon via Inagh. Stay on the N85 to get to Lahinch. Spanish Point is located about 13 km south of Lahinch. From Lahinch follow the signs for Miltown Malbay or Spanish Point. Some 2 km before reaching Miltown Malbay take a sharp turn to your left. Follow the road past the Armada hotel to reach the beach.

For public transport options check out the Bus Éireann (www.buseireann.ie) and Irish Rail (www.irishrail.ie) timetables.

Providers:

Surf schools in counties Sligo and Clare:

Perfect Day Surf School
Strandhill, Co. Sligo
Phone: +353 (0)71 91 28488/ +353 (0)87 202 9399
Email: info@perfectdaysurfing.com
Web: www.perfectdaysurfing.com

Seventh Wave Surf School
Enniscrone, Co. Sligo
Phone: +353 (0)87 971 6389
Email: seventhwavesurfschool@yahoo.co.uk
Web: www.seventhwavesurfschool.com

Strandhill Surf School,
Beach Stores, Strandhill, Co. Sligo
Phone: +353 (0)71 91 68483/+353 (0)87 287 0817
Email: strandhillsurfschool@eircom.net
Web: www.strandhillsurfschool.com

North West Surf School
Enniscorne, Co. Sligo
Phone: +353 (0)87 959 5556
Email: info@nwsurfschool.com
Web: www.nwsurfschool.com

Aloha Surf School
Fanore, Co. Clare
Phone: +353 (0)87 213 3996
Email: enquiries@surfschool.tv
Web: www.surfschool.tv

Ben's Surf Clinic
Lahinch, Co. Clare
Phone: +353 (0)86 844 8622,
Email: ben@benssurfclinic.com
Web: www.benssurfclinic.com

Lahinch Surf School
Ballyfaudeen, Lahinch, Co. Clare
Phone: +353 (0)65 708 2061, +353 (0) 87 960 9667 or +353 (0)65 708 2061
Email: lahinchsurfschool@eircom.net
Web: www.lahinchsurfschool.com

For more information about surfing in Ireland and a comprehensive list of surf schools and clubs; check out the Irish Surfing Association website www.isasurf.ie.

More about Surfing:

Surfing in Ireland doesn't exactly match the stereotypical image of waving palms, white sand and tropical blue sea.. But Ireland is known to have some of the best waves in Europe. If you're serious about surfing take a lesson at one of the many surfing schools around the country and buy yourself a board and a good winter wetsuit.

Safety:

Lahinch has some of the most dangerous currents in Ireland. Another danger is the weever fish that hide in the sand on the beach; in summer when the water is warm it is quite common to be stung, and the pain is excruciating if not treated properly. Contact a lifeguard immediately if stung.

o Never surf alone.
o If you are unfamiliar with a break talk with the lifeguards or locals about conditions. Until you gain a bit of experience stick to beaches and waves suitable to your ability.
o If you get caught in a rip current that takes you out to sea don't try to paddle against it. Paddle across the rip until you get out of it and then try to swim back to shore.
o Be aware of other surfers in the water. Never drop in on another surfer – the surfer closest the breaking part of the wave has priority.
o Respect surfing line-ups, where each surfer waits their turn to surf a wave.
o When you wipe out don't come to the surface too quickly; allow your board to surface before you surface.

For more information about safety and surfing etiquette see www.isasurf.ie.

Accommodation

Enniscrone and Easkey:

Atlantic Caravan Park (atlanticcaravanpk@eircom.net, +353 (0)96 36132), located beside the beach in Enniscrone, is the perfect place to pitch a tent. LJ's hostel (+353 (0)86 815 4400), right in Easkey town, is another popular option for surfers on a budget.

For more accommodation options in Sligo check out the accommodation section on www.sligotourism.ie.

Lahinch and Spanish Point:

Lahinch hostel (+353 (0)65 708 1040) offers dorm beds at €15 per person and private/family rooms from €20–40 per night. Full equipped bungalows located close to the beach can be rented from Spanish Point Holiday Homes (www.tridentholidayhomes.ie, +353 (0)87 942 6935).

For more accommodation options check out www.discoverireland.ie, www.lahinchfailte.com, www.sligotourism.ie.

Other attractions:

After a long day surfing in Easkey or Enniscrone be sure to call into the Kilcullen seaweed baths

(+353 (0)96 36238) in Enniscrone. The therapeutic power of the seaweed bath is attributed to the high concentration of iodine that occurs naturally in sea water and seaweed.

Easkey is also well known as a prime location for both surf kayaking and river kayaking. In 2003 the village hosted the world kayaking championships. You can also try your hand at fishing for salmon on the Easkey river; the required fishing licence can be purchased at Fordes shop.

Just north of Lahinch, on the coast of west Clare, are the very popular Cliffs of Moher. There are spectacular views of the Aran islands and the Clare coastline from the 8-km long and up to 215metre high sea cliffs. The cliffs can be visited daily all year round, but be prepared to pay high parking costs at the car park. In 2005 perfect conditions allowed a group of surfers for the first time to surf the infamous giant wave 'Aill Na Searrach' crashing at the foot of the cliffs. The adventure has been captured in a documentary about surfing culture in Ireland called *And Then the Wind Died.*

Lahinch is also close to the Burren, a unique karst-limestone landscape covering 250 km of northwest county Clare. The Burren contains some of Ireland's best examples of megalithic tombs, ring forts and portal dolmens. If you have the time try to spend at least a day on one of the Aran islands; ferries leave daily from Doolin, 17 km north of Lahinch. There are plenty of good snorkelling and scuba diving locations in Clare (see chapter: Snorkelling – Kilkee, Co. Clare).

Best time to go/season:

The best time is between September and May when swells are at their best. The water temperature tends to be quite low during this time of the year so bring a thick 6mm wetsuit and a hot flask of tea. Summer surfing can be a bit crowded but water temperatures are more welcoming.

Links:

www.isasurf.ie;
www.magicseaweed.com;
www.met.ie.

WHALE WATCHING
UNION HALL, CO. CORK

We drove to Reen pier outside Union Hall and arrived just in time to meet the morning passengers as they disembarked. I was relieved to note the enthusiasm in their voices, as my previous attempts at whale watching had been less than fruitful. We were fitted with life jackets as we boarded the boat, then Nic Slocum gave us a quick but comprehensive safety briefing as we headed out to sea.

The day, although grey, was perfect for whale watching. The sea was flat calm which made it easy to see whenever the surface was broken; the calm conditions allowed us to see several miles in all directions. Nic told us to look out for large flocks of birds as an indicator of whale feeding activity. He pointed out 'whale footprints' – areas of flat slick spots of still water sometimes indicative of a whale just beneath the surface. He also explained the difference between the two species of whales that they had been lucky enough to spot in recent weeks. The fin whale, a baleen whale, is the second largest animal on Earth (after

the blue whale), weighing in at 30–80 tonnes. It emits a distinctive noise as it expels air through its blowhole; the water lodged in the blowhole is expelled in a columnar blow into the air. Nic went on to explain that on a grey day on a grey sea against a background of grey rock it might be difficult to see the blow, but on this occasion we were not to be disappointed. Again the conditions favoured us as, not only could we see over large distances, but the sound of the blow travelled well over the water on the calm day. Our first sighting was not of a fin but of a minke whale, the smallest and most abundant baleen whale. Minke whales grow to about 25–30 feet long and up to 14 tonnes in weight. They start exhaling before they reach the surface, which means their blow is inconspicuous when compared to some other whales.

A short time later we were rewarded with out first sighting of a fin whale. We had been looking out for flocks of birds, as advised by Nic, but nothing can prepare you for the noise and the mania surrounding the feeding as the birds descend. It sounded like a primary school playground, with loud shrieks as birds fought over the spoils. Then as quickly as they descended they disappeared and all was quiet again. It was amazing to watch. The birds later tipped us off to one of the most spectacular sights of the day – a whale lunge feeding. The birds took flight just as the whale's jaws broke the surface of the water only metres from the boat. Nic explained that we could only see at best 25 per cent of the whale over the surface. What we saw was immense, the whale's huge size totally dwarfing the 30 ft boat. We thought about the times we had kayaked these waters and wondered how we might have reacted if one of these majestic creatures surfaced beside us. It's surprising how excited people get when they see the smallest portion of the animal break the surface – all those onboard moved from one side of the boat to the other as whales were spotted. We each became more animated as the whales began surfacing in different areas. Nic has been spotting whales for twenty-five years and it was clear to see that he still finds it incredibly exciting. He believes that for viewing aquatic life, Ireland is 'world class', and this season (2007) in West Cork has been as good as it gets. His excitement is infectious. Speaking passionately about marine tourism, he punctuates his sentences with 'minke' and 'fin', pointing out the various whales in the vicinity. There were, at that time, eight minke whales, six fin whales and dozens of dolphins in the area. Nic

and his wife Wendy are conservationists who follow the WDCS Cetacean Watching Code of Conduct, which includes suggestions on how close to get, how much time to spend with the animals and how to manoeuvre the boat. We were fortunate enough to have dolphins escort us for some of the trip; they swam and jumped playfully alongside and underneath the boat. While the whales were majestic, for some the energetic and playful dolphin performance was the highlight of the trip.

It is difficult to capture the magic of a trip like this in words or with a photograph. It is a peak experience and it's on your doorstep. This is one not to be missed.

Getting there:

The RV *Voyager* leaves from Reen pier, Castlehaven, west Cork. Reen pier is about 3 km from Union Hall village. Union Hall is 77 km west of Cork City. Take the N71 out of Cork city and continue through Bandon and then Clonakilty. About 15 km outside Clonakilty turn left, following signs for Union Hall and then Reen pier. Bus Éireann runs a service from Cork city to nearby Leap and Skibbereen. Check www.buseireann.ie for the latest timetable (route 237 or 252).

The area:

The small port town of Union hall is located in the heart of West Cork. The village is surrounded by extensive woodland and overlooks the Glandore Harbour. The busy fishing port is popular with sea anglers and cruise boats.

Provider:

Whale Watch West Cork (www.whalewatch-westcork.com, +353 (0)86 120 0027, +353 (0)28 33357) runs whale watching boat trips all year round. The tour lasts between three and four hours.

Low season tour: 10 a.m., 2 p.m.; High season (July, August): 5.30 a.m., 9.15 a.m., 1 p.m. Price: Adults: €50, children €35

West Cork Marine Tours (www.whales-dolphins-ireland.com, +353 (0)86 327 3226). The tour lasts four hours and leaves the pier at 10 a.m. or 3 p.m. Adults €40, children €30.

More about whale watching:

Irish waters are among Europe's richest for cetaceans, with an impressive twenty-four species recorded to date. In 1991 the Irish government accepted an IWDG proposal, declaring Ireland a whale and dolphin sanctuary – the first of its kind in Europe. People travel to Ireland from all around the world to see whales. Various species are regularly spotted off the Irish coast, including the fin whale, the second largest species in the world at over 80 tonnes.

For more information about whale watching in Ireland check out the Irish Whale and Dolphin website www.iwdg.ie.

Accommodation:

Accommodation in the area includes Atlantic House in Castletownsend (www.atlantichouse-accommodation.com, +353 (0) 28 36440), a B&B with rooms for €30–35 pp sharing, Inish Beg self-catering cottages (www.inishbeg.com, +353 (0)28 21745), and Bushe's bar overlooking Baltimore harbour (www.bushesbar.com, +353 (0)28 20125), which has doubles from €55 a night. For more accommodation options check out www.discoverireland.com.

Other attractions:

West Cork is rich in natural beauty and cultural activities. Try sea kayaking (see chapter: Sea Kayaking - Castleisland, West Cork), cycle the ring of Bera, visit Ireland's most southwesterly point at Mizen head signal station visitor centre or attend one of the many summer West Cork festivals. For more information about the West Cork region check out www.discoverireland.com.

Best time to go/season:

Dolphins and porpoises can be spotted off Co. Cork all year round. Dolphin numbers peak around the winter solstice, when you might see 2–3,000 dolphins at a time. Whales tend to be more seasonal, resident in Cork from June to January.

Links:

www.whalewatchwestcork.com;
www.iwdg.ie (Irish Whale and Dolphin Group);
www.westcork.ie;
www.cork-guide.ie.

MOUNTAIN BIKING
BALLYHOURA, CO. LIMERICK

We decided to herald the first day of the Irish winter and its predictably unpredictable weather with a visit to the Ballyhoura mountain park. Having completely ignored the weather forecasts and ominous grey sky we were delighted to arrive to a dry greenwood forest car park and see it full of cars with bike racks. We put on our rain jackets and helmets and headed towards what is soon to be the Ballyhoura mountain bike centre.

I should state at the outset that I own the cleanest mountain bike in Ireland. It had never been off road; nor, for that matter, had I. As we progressed uphill (slowly in my case) the panoramic view became more spectacular. Stretched out below us was a mixed canvas

of rugged mountain gorse, woodland, moor, peat bog and farmland, a vista that is sure to impress the thousands of riders who will surely visit this centre. Very quickly we found ourselves removed from the road below us. As the trails were not officially open when we visited we decided to embrace the spirit of adventure and explore some of the trails. When we moved off the forest roads we quickly learned that single track means just that – in places there is barely enough room for the bike to pass through. I found myself putting my legs out to either side like I had just got my stabilisers off for fear of catching my pedals off the rocks and stumps which lined the path. The ride is exhilarating; you are constantly watching for obstacles in your path, correcting for wind or trying to pedal yourself out of a mud patch that seems unreasonably deep. I had to dismount on more than one occasion, terrified of falling over the edge of the path as I peddled through driving rain. At one stage, unsure of our route, we were exploring a trail when a group of riders came careering down the trail at speed. One came off his bike and was back on so quickly we weren't even sure it had happened. His friends, however, didn't miss the novice mistake; the jeering and laughter followed them down slope at speed. I was glad they hadn't seen me pushing my shiny bike a little earlier. We reached a narrow wooden pathway which crossed a small waterfall. I baulked again, but it didn't deter my fellow rider, who sped over this narrow boardwalk, loving every second. The rain began to pelt down as we progressed onto another part of the trail which seemed to have strategically placed rocks which allowed just enough room to turn the wheel and prevent you from careering headfirst into a tree. At this point we went our separate ways, the more adventurous rider opting to try out some more challenging terrain, the less adventurous opting to retrace the same route home. Then all at once the predictions of the weather forecasters proved devastatingly accurate; as I sped down the path the rain seemed to defy gravity and lash horizontally at me. This was nothing, however, compared to the hailstones that clipped my ears for the next ten minutes. The sound of hailstones smacking off my helmet while high winds rushed through the trees actually heightened the experience – the adrenaline was really pumping by the time I left the trail. Feeling braver with the single track behind me, I raced the run-off down the forest road back to the car, but my fear increased with my speed. It wasn't until I began to feel pain in my arms that I realised I had a death grip on the handlebars. I've a lot to learn but I'm looking forward to the return visit.

We learned first-hand that this trail system caters for novices and experts alike. It ranges from gentle climbs and exciting descents to challenging climbs with technical single-track descents. This is an exhilarating, accessible, all-weather activity. Go on, get on your bike.

Getting there:

The mountain biking trails start and end at the Mountain Biking Centre near Ardpatrick in Co. Limerick. Ardpatrick is located 75 km north-west of Cork city, 41 km southeast of Limerick, 60 km from Shannon, 145 km from Galway and 226 km from Dublin.

From Limerick take the Killmallock road (R512) through Bruff to Kilmallock. Turn left in the village, following signs for Blackpool and Ardpatrick (R512). From Cork city take the N8 through Fermoy to Mitchelstown, and from there take the N73 to Kildorrery. Turn right in Kildorrery, following signs for Ardpatrick. The Mountain Biking Centre is approximately 5 km outside Ardpatrick; on the R512 take a right turn signposted Castleoliver view and from here follow the signs for the centre.

The area:

Ballyhoura park is a natural park which covers an area of approx. 10,000 hectares. It is well known to walkers and orienteering enthusiasts, as there are marked walks, trails and courses for all abilities. However, the cycle track looks set to steal the limelight with outdoor adventurers, can look forward to a true wilderness biking experience.

Provider:

The Mountain Biking Centre near Ardpatrick opened in March 2008. A range of visitor services are provided, including bike hire, car parking, bike wash, showers and toilets. Use of the trails are free, with small charges applying to the other services provided. Fore more information see www.ballyhouramtb.com.

More about Mountain Biking

The mountain bike trails are a bike rider's dream, with three world-class trails, 91 km in total of way-marked routes using a combination of forest roads and newly built single-track

trails. The trail system was designed by the world's leading trail designer, Dafydd Davis, who has created some of the most exciting and challenging trails known to mountain bikers across the globe. There are three trails in all, with each of the circular loops offering a different experience, length and level of difficulty.

o Loop 1 – 16 km: short and almost entirely on single tracks which climb gently and have exciting but not too technical descents.
o Loop 2 – 27 km: moderate length with more challenging climbs. The majority of the trail is single track with approx 7 km on forest road.
o Loop 3 – 48 km: a long trail with most of the climbs on forest roads and all of the descents on single track.

For a comprehensive list of cycling clubs in Ireland check out the club directory on www.cyclingireland.ie.

Accommodation:

For accommodation in Ardpatrick try Castlemoor B&B (+353 (0)61 331802). Ballyhoura Country View (+353 (0)86 604 8993) and Beach Grove (+353 (0)61 355493) provide self-catering accommodation. B&Bs in Kilfinane include Woodview B&B (+353 (0)63 91106, Glebe Road, Kilfinane). St Andrews villa (+353 (0)63 91008, Kilfinane) and Lantern Lodge (+353 (0)63 91085, Ballyorgan, Kilfinane). For a list of accommodation options in the Ballyhoura area

check out the accommodation section on www.
ballyhouracountry.com or contact the Kilfinane
tourist office at + 353 (0)63 91300.

Other attractions:

Hill walking is popular in and around Ballyhoura. The Ballyhoura international walking festival
takes place every May with organised walks on
one of the twenty routes in the area, including
the Ballyhoura Way. The Beast of Ballyhoura adventure race (www.ballyhourabeast.com) takes
place in August. Running continuously over
twenty-two to twenty-eight hours, it involves
mountain biking, orienteering, mountaineering,
abseiling, kayaking and shooting.

The Kilfinane Outdoor Education Centre
provide a range of outdoor activities including
canoeing, kayaking, rock climbing, horse riding, orienteering, hill walking and river walking (see chapter: River Walking – Kilfinane,
Co. Limerick).

Best time to go/season:

Any time of the year.

Links:

www.ballyhouramtb.com;
www.cyclingireland.ie;
www.kilfinaneoec.com;
www.ballyhouracountry.com;
www.visitlimerick.com;
www.ballyhoura.com;
www.discoverireland.com;
www.irishdh.com
www.mtbrider.com.

MOONLIGHT SEA KAYAKING
KINSALE, CO. CORK

Having missed the ideal night paddle opportunity on an August full moon, we were determined to get out on the water for the September full moon. The night came and, although conditions were not as appealing as the previous month, we decided to go for it. It was a chilly night and so we donned our less than attractive thermal long johns – one of the many reasons why it was best for us to do this at night! We set off from Cork for Kinsale, congratulating ourselves on our spirit of adventure. Thirty minutes later we were second-guessing the decision to abandon the TV for the night. The night air was cold and as the tide was particularly low we had to negotiate a very slimy boat slip to get the kayaks into the water. The cold night and precarious entry coupled with the overpowering smell of sewage had taken the romantic edge off our plan. However, we persevered.

Kinsale is generally a very busy town, hugely popular with tourists. As a result there is rarely a time where the town is not congested with traffic. Not so at night, however, which makes it a pleasure to paddle there in the quieter evenings. It also provides options, as there are a number of places where the kayaks can be put in. You can paddle up the Bandon river to Kilmacsimon or, if feeling very energetic, to Inishannon, or you can paddle around the marina or out to sea through the harbour.

There is a burgeoning sailing community in the town with two active marinas. There is also a thriving fishing industry, which means that the water can be as busy as the streets at times – another reason why the night paddle is a great option.

Kinsale harbour is a safe sheltered location for paddling; however, as with all water sports, safety comes first. We were both wearing a thermal layer, a cag, booties and a buoyancy aid. Our buoyancy aids had high visibility reflective strips. In addition we wore head torches, although the moonlight was sufficient to light our path.

We parked at a slip located on the western side of the harbour and unloaded the boats. We made our way slowly down the slip; unfortunately, however, when we got to the bottom the tide was so low we had to step through the slob (muddy, smelly sludge) to get the boats to the water. This done, we set off on our paddle. There was an eerie quality to the night, with no wind and almost no movement on the water. We slowly paddled towards the marina by the Dock bar, checking out some of the sailboats as we moved effortlessly through the water. We spotted a sailboat listing to one side; on closer investigation it seemed to be caught on a sandbank. Our curiosity caused us to separate out on the water, but only until a dark shadow passed under my boat. It didn't take me long to paddle back to company. The shadow passed again and, just as I was about to freak out, my paddle struck the ground. The tide was so low the bottom of the kayak was touching the seabed. A gentle reminder that you never know what to expect on the water. Having paddled numerous times around Kinsale we never experienced tides as low. Some internet research revealed that the September full moons are called harvest moons and that what we experienced was a spring tide (which has nothing to do with the season). Apparently on a full moon the gravitational pull of the moon and sun are combined, causing low tides to be very low. Whatever the reason I was glad it was only seaweed. On other night paddles we have been lucky to experience phosphorescence shimmering brilliantly under the kayaks, but each trip offers something different. We paddled by the ruins of James fort and around by Jarley's cove out to Money point. From there we pointed the nose of the boats towards Charles fort, a seventeenth-century star fort which is well worth a visit. The view from Charles fort over Kinsale is impressive by day and by night. We just sat in the boats, the sea and air motionless around us, and soaked up the atmosphere under the full moon. Getting the gear together and loading up the boats at night takes a bit of effort, but in our experience the night paddle always rewards that effort.

Getting there:

By Car:
Kinsale is located 27km from Cork city, 21km from Cork airport and 22km from Cork ferryport (Ringaskiddy). Blarney is 39 km away, Killarney 87 km and Cobh (via harbour ferry) 32 km.

From Cork city follow the signs for Cork airport. At the roundabout at the entrance to the airport take the second exit (R600) and follow this road for about 20 km through the villages of Riverstick and Belgooly and into Kinsale.

Public Transport: Cork city is well served by both train and bus. The Bus Éireann number 249 travels frequently between Cork bus station and Kinsale. Check www.buseireann.ie or call Bus Éireann on +353 (0)21 450 8188 for the latest timetable.

The area:
Kinsale is located at the mouth of the Bandon River. Kinsale is a tradional commercial port with a long history. The two imposing forts, Charles fort and James fort overlooking the harbour indicate the strategic importance Kinsale once had. Kinsale is now popular with sailing enthusiasts. The sheltered harbour has two fully serviced ma-

rinas, during the summer months they tend to be packed with pleasure boats.

Provider:

Both H2O Sea Kayaking (www.h2oseakayaking.com, +353 (0)21 477 8884) and the Kinsale Outdoor Education Centre (www.kinsaleoutdoors.com, +353 (0)21 477 2896) offer canoe and kayak courses to all levels in the Kinsale area. All kayaking equipment is provided. You will need to bring swimming togs/shorts, a towel, a pair of trainers/sandals that you don't mind getting wet, a sun hat/sun cream and a water bottle.

More about kayaking:

Kinsale harbour is just one of many kayaking locations in the area. You can also kayak around Sandycove Island (see chapter: Sea Kayaking – Sandycove, Cork), around Oysterhaven bay, up or down the Bandon river or out around the old head of Kinsale. Diverse wildlife can be spotted in the waters around Kinsale, including seals, whales, dolphins, porpoise and an array of sea birds.

Accommodation:

Guardwell hostel in Kinsale (www.kinsalehostel.com, +353 (0)21 477 4686), Dempseys hostel (+353 (0)21 477 2124), Trident hotel (www.tridenthotel.com, +353 (0)21 477 2301), Actons hotel (www.actonshotelkinsale.com, +353 (0)21 277 2135). For more accommodation options in the Kinsale area check out www.kinsale.ie/kinsacco.htm, or

call the Kinsale tourist office on +353 (0)21 477 2234. For accommodation options in the Cork area contact the Cork tourist office on +353 (0)21 427 3251.

Other attractions:

Kinsale is famous for its gourmet food, art and craft shops and range of leisure activities. Two festivals, Kinsale arts week in early July and the Kinsale food festival in October justifiably attract large crowds. There are plenty of tourist attractions in the Kinsale area. Charles fort, built in 1677, is a classic example of a star-shaped fort and boasts panoramic views of Kinsale harbour. The old head of Kinsale is now home to an exclusive golf course, and access to the head is restricted to club members. You can, however, park at the entrance to the golf club car park and get a good view of the old head by venturing either east or west from the golf club entrance. Popular activities in the area include sailing, sea angling, surfing (see chapter: Bodyboarding - Garretstown, Cork) and whale watching. Check out www.kinsale.ie for a list of activity providers.

Best time to go/season:

Full moon any time of the year.

Links:

www.kinsale.ie;
www.corkkerry.ie
www.irishislands.info
www.atlanticseakayaking.com
www.irishcanoeunion.com
www.kinsaletimes.com.

SNORKELLING,
KILKEE, CO. CLARE

The crystal clear waters of the Atlantic ocean, an abundance of marine life and the naturally sheltered Kilkee bay provide an ideal snorkelling and diving location. Three natural rock pools located within the Duggerne reef on the south-western side of the bay are called the pollock holes and are a popular shallow sheltered snorkelling location. The north-western shore of the bay below the golf course is also quite good, providing deeper water to surface dive with plenty of caves to explore.

With this in mind we headed for Clare and set up our tents on a large grass bank overlooking the northern tip of Kilkee bay. We awoke to a clear blue sky and a flat calm sea, ideal snorkelling conditions. There were numerous early risers walking the cliff path and playing golf on the Kilkee golf course behind us. As none of us had snorkelled on this side of Kilkee bay before, we first decided to explore the coast, scouting good snorkelling locations. The cliff path rose quickly, giving amazing views along the rugged Clare coastline. After a couple of near misses with golf balls we happened upon a few caves and reefs worth exploring.

It was early September yet there were numerous swimmers braving the cold water in the flesh. Not us, though; we carried all the gear down to the small stone beach below us and suited up. There were four of us so we decided to pair off using the buddy system to keep an eye on each other. This safety system is designed to ensure you and your buddy are responsible for each other's safety and can raise the alarm quickly should one of you get into trouble.

In no time we were in the water exploring the coastline and venturing into the many rock enclaves. The visibility was quite good but the water was deep in sections, requiring you to surface dive in places to see anything. I had opted for warmth over manoeuvrability, so the buoyancy of my wetsuit was keeping me from surface diving to any great depth. We made our way north along the coast across a shallow rock face, spotting sea urchins and small fish along the way. An hour into the trip we began to feel the cold so we made our way back towards the beach, passing over an amazing section of long tagliatelle-like seaweed swaying with the changing tide.

It's an incredible feeling to be below the surface of the sea moving with ease among fascinating sea creatures, forests of seaweed, underwater cliffs and caves with only the sound of your own breathing for company. It's a special experience, which requires no specialist training, very little equipment and just a little adventurous spirit.

Getting there:

Situated in Co. Clare on the west coast of Ireland, Kilkee is easily accessed by both road and air. Shannon airport is located 72 km (65 minutes' drive) directly inland (www.shannon-airport.com). Daily bus services link Kilkee with all major cities and towns in Ireland while roads connect Kilkee with Ennis (56 km), Limerick (92 km), Galway (123 km), Cork (193 km) and Dublin (290 km). The frequency of bus services increases during the summer season. Check out www.buseireann.ie for timetables. The nearest train station is Ennis; check www.irishrail.com for the latest Dubln to Ennis timetable.

If driving from Dublin take the N7 to Limerick. From Limerick take the N18 towards Ennis; follow signs for the N68 to Kilrush and from there take the signposted road to Kilkee.

The area:

Kilkee is a popular seaside resort due mainly to the mile-long horseshoe Moore bay. The blue flag beach in the town and the 13-metre diving boards and natural swimming pools at 'new found out' are popular hangouts during the summer. The entrance to the bay is protected by a natural reef known as Duggerne reef.

Provider:

The Kilkee Dive Centre is located 200 metres from the jetty. The centre is a PADI gold palm dive centre and an ISA training centre. The training centre is open from Easter until the end of October with diving every day, weather permitting. The dive centre is fully equipped with changing rooms, showers, rental equipment, washing facilities, compressor and an onsite dive shop (www.oceanlife.ie, +353 (0)65 905 6707).

More about snorkelling

To snorkel you will need a mask, snorkel, fins and, optionally, a wetsuit. If you are serious about taking up snorkelling and eventually moving onto scuba diving you should take a snorkelling course with one of the many Irish scuba diving clubs registered with Comhairle Fo-Thuinn (the Irish underwater council www.cft.ie).

You should never snorkel alone and when in an unfamiliar area ask locals about conditions, safe locations and those to be avoided.

Other popular snorkelling areas in Co. Clare include the Bridges of Ross and around Crab island in Doolin. Doolin has become a popular diving location, particularly following

the discovery in the 1980s of a network of sub-marine caves off Doolin point. These were named the Green Holes of Doolin and some 1,250 metres have been charted.

Accommodation:

Kilkee can be particularly busy during the summer months so book well in advance. Cunningham's holiday park (+353 (0)65 905 6430) located within the town and Green Acres caravan and camping park (+353 (0)65 905 7011) located 6 km south of Kilkee along the R487 offer camping facilities. Katie O'Connor's hostel located 14 km away in Kilrush is the nearest hostel (+353 (0)65 905 1133).

For a comprehensive list of accommodation options in Kilkee check out the accommodation listings on www.discoverireland.ie

or call the Kilkee tourist office (open only during the summer months) at +353 (0)65 905 6112 or the Ennis tourist office at +353 (0)65 682 8366 or 682 8308.

Other attractions:

Nearby Lahinch and Spanish point are popular surfing destinations (see the chapter; Surfing - Sligo and Clare). Loop head, a well signposted drive takes you south of Kilkee along a dramatic cliff route through picturesque villages.

The Bridges of Ross, south of Kilkee near the village of Cross, is famous for the naturally formed rock bridges sculpted by the eroding power of the Atlantic ocean. The weaker rock has been gradually worn away by the sea over the centuries, leaving behind long tunnels covered by thin layers of topsoil and rock; this topsoil caved in places, leaving the famous 'Bridges of Ross'.

Boat trips from Kilrush (www.discoverdolphins.ie +353 (0)65 905 1327) or Carrigaholt (www.dolphinwatch.ie +353 (0)65 905 8156) offer dolphin-watching cruises along the Shannon estuary. Further north a friendly dolphin known locally as 'Fáinne' or 'Dusty' frequents the waters around Fanore. The dolphin has been known to swim with locals on occasion. Check out www.irishdolphins.com for more information.

The Cliffs of Moher, one of Ireland's most visited tourist attractions, are located north of Lahinch along the R478. Further north again is the unique Burren landscape, a karst-limestone region measuring 250 square kilometres. The area is filled with historical and archaeological sites; for more information check out www.burrenbeo.ie.

The fifteenth-century Bunratty castle is located just off the main dual carriageway (N18) between Shannon and Limerick. Guided tours of the castle and folk park are available all year round. Medieval-style banquets are held twice every evening (5.30 p.m. and 8.45 p.m.) in the great hall.

Best time to go/season:

It's possible to snorkel or dive all year round but for bearable water temperatures any time between May and September.

Links:

www.cft.ie;
www.loopheadclare.com;
www.oceanlife.ie;
www.aaallaboutwestclare.com;
www.kilkee.ie.

HILL WALKING
CARRAUNTOOHIL, CO. KERRY

It was 5.30 in the evening and the sun was still extremely hot; it had been one of the hottest days of the year. We set off from the car with a bag full of clothes, water and food.

There are a number of routes to the summit. We decided to take Brother O'Shea's gully route, one of the longer but more scenic routes. A warning notice from Kerry county council greeted us at the start of the walk - It's a 'people who don't take heed of this notice will die a painful death' type of notice. Well not quite but It does serve as an important reminder to be prepared for all types of weather and hiking conditions. The first half hour was on relatively flat open ground running parallel to a winding shallow stream. A few hikers greeted us on their way down, the ground was marshy in places and I'm told it can get wet and slippery in poor weather conditions. We took a break beside a mountain stream and looked down on Lough Gouragh and Lough Callee.

The ascent started to become a lot steeper; the shirts came off and the sweat was pumping. Underfoot the stones gave way easily, I needed to concentrate on every step. In places we used our hands to climb but in general the ascent was pretty manageable. Brother O'Shea's gully route is not marked, but my guide has climbed this route several times and stopped at regular intervals to check his bearings. We reached Cummeenoughter Lake, reputed to be the highest in Ireland. It wasn't quite the cobalt blue colour I had expected, more like a green pool of mud.

Nearing the top, it started to get very

steep; I began to regret the decision not to wear hiking boots. At the col at the top of the slope we were rewarded with an amazing view down into Coomloughra, with Dingle Bay and the Brandon group to the Northwest. A short walk along an exposed ridge delivered us to the summit. We reached the cross at the top and absorbed the spectacular view. My guide had been to the summit several times but had never experienced these near perfect conditions. It was absolutely breath taking.

From the summit we followed a well-trodden stone path in a south easterly direction. This path is part of the popular devils ladder route. The path known as the ramp was unclear as we veered off to our left following

the contours of the mountain in a in a north easterly direction towards a very steep section aptly named the heavenly gates. I took my time along here, realising that any wrong step could be the end of my days.

Continuing down the mountain we passed an emergency hut on our left. The decent was tricky in places but we eventually rejoined the Brother O'Sheas gully trail that took us up the mountain. Back on familiar ground it took us another thirty minutes to get back to the car. While my feet were burning and my body tired my first ascent of Ireland's highest summit was worth every ache.

Getting there:

Carrauntoohil is located close to Killarney town in the southwest of Ireland. Killarney is served by national primary route N22 (north to Tralee and Castleisland, south to Cork) and national secondary route N72 (west to Killorglin, east to Waterford). There are train services to Tralee, Limerick, Cork and Dublin operated by Iarnród Éireann (www.irishrail.ie). Bus Éireann provides bus services to Limerick (and onwards to Dublin), Tralee, Cork, Kenmare and Skibbereen (www.buseireann.ie). Kerry international airport, in Farranfore between Tralee and Killarney, provides an increasing number of air services.

The easiest starting point for climbing

Carrauntoohil is from Cronin's yard, (www. croninsyard.com), situated at the base of the Macgillycuddy Reeks just twenty minutes from Killarney town. To reach Cronin's yard take the N72 (Ring of Kerry road) from Killarney, turn left for Gap of Dunloe and continue on this road for approximately 8 km until you come to a sign pointing left for Carrauntoohil. Proceed to the end of this road.

The area:

Carrauntoohil is the highest peak in Ireland (1,040 metres) and is the central peak of the Macgillycuddy Reeks range, a rugged twelve-mile ridge which stretches along the south-west corner of Ireland. The existing metal cross on the summit was erected in 1976 to replace the previous wooden one which was erected in 1950. The surface of the cross has a blackened charred appearance as a result of numerous lightning strikes.

More about hill walking

The route chosen involved ascending via Brother O'Sheas gully route and descending via the heavenly gates. This is the second most popular route on Carrauntoohill, the most popular route being the devil's ladder'. The route can become quite congested during the summer; allow six hours for the round trip and be prepared for all types of weather, whatever the conditions when you first set off.

This route should only be attempted by experienced climbers in conjunction with one of these maps:

- Harvey 'Superwalker' 1:30,000 'MacGillycuddy's Reeks'
- Ordnance Survey Ireland 1:50,000 Discovery Series Sheet 78
- Ordnance Survey Ireland 1:25,000 Map 'MacGillycuddy's Reeks'

There are several routes up the mountain; for a detailed outline of three of these routes, along with important safety precautions, check out www.kerrymountainrescue.ie. The book Carrauntoohil & MacGillycuddy's Reeks by Jim Ryan outlines several other routes up the mountain.

For more information about hill walking in Ireland and a comprehensive list of hill walking clubs; contact the Mountaineering Council of Ireland at (+353 (0)1 625 1115) or check out their website www.mountaineering.ie.

Accommodation:

Killarney is the best place to base yourself when climbing Carrauntoohil. The town is a popular tourist destination and has plenty of accommodation options available. Hostels: Killarney Railway hostel (+353 (0)64 35299), Killarney international youth hostel (+353 (0)64 31240), Park hostel (+353 (0)64 32119).

Hotels:

There are numerous hotels available. These include Riverside hotel (+353 (0)64 39200), Lake hotel (+353 (0)64 31035), located on the lakeshore, and Killarney Court hotel (+353 (0)64 37070), to name but a few.

For a complete list of accommodation op-

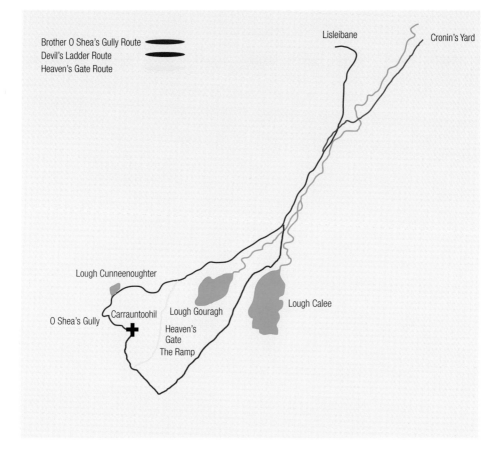

Brother O Shea's Gully Route
Devil's Ladder Route
Heaven's Gate Route

Lisleibane

Cronin's Yard

Lough Cunneenoughter

Lough Calee

O Shea's Gully

Carrauntoohil

Lough Gouragh

Heaven's
Gate
The Ramp

tions in the Kerry region check out the www. corkkerry.ie accommodation guide.

Other attractions:

There are plenty of other activities and sites to see in the Killarney area: Walking routes in the area include the 215 km Kerry way (www. kerryway.net), the 179 km Dingle way (www. dingleway.net) and the 197 km Beara way (www.bearaway.net). For information on way-marked walking trails in Ireland see www. walkireland.ie. Popular tourist sites in the Kerry area include the circular 170 km Ring of Kerry tourist trail, the Lakes of Killarney, Mount Brandon, and the Blasket islands (see www.blasketislands.ie or www.blasketisland. com for ferry times).

Historic sites include Eightercua; a mega-lithic tomb, Muckross house (www.muckross-house.ie) , Ross castle, Gallarus oratory; an early Christian church and Skellig Michael; the larger of the two skellig islands (see www. skelligexperience.com for ferry times).

Best time to go/season:

June to September.

Links:

www.corkkerry.ie
www.kerrymountainrescue.ie.

RIVER WALKING
KILFINANE, CO. LIMERICK

For nine years we've been travelling with school groups to Kilfinane Outdoor Education Centre in Co. Limerick. For the first few years there was no mention of river walking so when I first heard it mentioned four years ago I was intrigued. We've never looked back. It's now consistently the most popular activity with students.

River walking is just that – walking in a river. It's also known as canyoning and more commonly in Ireland as gorge walking. Gorge walking involves walking in the path of a river, slipping and scrambling over rocks, climbing waterfalls and jumping or sliding off them, traversing across and plunging into pools. It involves elements of climbing, swimming and walking. More than anything it's a very enjoyable activity which is accessible to everyone in this country, it's suitable for all ages and abilities and is surprisingly satisfying. It's a great year-round activity (with a decent wetsuit) because if you've decided to go river walking you've already accepted that you will get wet and probably fall a lot – the weather isn't really a factor.

We put on wetsuits, buoyancy aids and helmets and headed off for a local river. Accessing the river involves a short trip by minibus from the village of Kilfinane to a tributary of the Loobagh river. After parking the instructor took a few minutes to check all the equipment was being worn correctly, helmets were on and the straps on the buoyancy aids were tight. Some of the group were non-swimmers, but this did not prevent them from taking part fully. The wetsuits and buoyancy aids keep swimmers and non-swimmers afloat, but there was still a little trepidation as we set off down a farm track. Five minutes later we crossed a small bridge where we caught our first glimpse of the river; all anxiety was quickly dispelled as we entered the river at ankle height. We made our way carefully over the slippery rocks. The instructor was quick to get the entire group into the water so our wetsuits would keep us warm. We clambered over the first obstacle, which was a small waterfall, and moved on to the next shallow section of river. It was difficult to tell whether the water was shallow or deep, which made for great entertainment. At some stages you are negotiating with sandy-bottomed ankle-height water and then you're into waist-high water on a rocky river bed. I have done this walk six times now and the river is always different. The instructor explained that after a period of heavy rain there can be a really strong flow of water and that it can be a real battle to make your way upstream. After a few hundred metres the group reached a narrow passage where the water was about waist height; they pushed their way through, laughing at those who stumbled (survival of the fittest). When we reached the waterfall there was a free-for-all swim in the plunge pool while the instructor scrambled up the bank to secure a rope for those who wished to climb the waterfall and then jump off. A few brave souls showered under the waterfall while the others waited for their turn to climb. The rope proved necessary, as the waterfall was very slippery and difficult

to negotiate, but for some this only enhanced the challenge. Those who made it to the top then took a moment to psyche themselves up. The jump is the highlight for many but even for those who don't face the plunge, river walking is a peak experience that is well worth a try.

Getting there:

The Kilfinane Outdoor Education Centre is situated in the village of Kilfinane, Co. Limerick. Kilfinane is 72 km north-west of Cork, 41 km southeast of Limerick, 59 km from Shannon, 145 km from Galway and 216 km from Dublin.

From Limerick take the Killmallock road (R512) through Bruff to Kilmallock. Turn left in Kilmallock, following signs for Kilfinane (R517). From Cork city take the N8 through Fermoy to Mitchelstown, and from there follow signs for Kilfinane.

Provider:

The Kilfinane Outdoor Education Centre (www. kilfinaneoec.com, +353 (0)63 91161/91059) provide outdoor education courses for school, youth and adult groups and a range of adventure sport courses for individuals (adults). Activities offered include canoeing, kayaking, river walking, rock climbing, abseiling, hill walking, orienteering, and horse riding.

More about River Walking:

River Walking gear includes climbing hardware, static ropes, wetsuits and specially designed shoes, packs, and rope bags. The Kilfinane outdoor adventure centre provides all the specialised gear, although you will need to bring a swimsuit/togs, towel and an old pair of shoes. Groups of twelve people are taken river walking, six people when the river is high.

Hazards include flash floods, underwater currents, rocks, hypothermia and potholes, all of which can be avoided by using the appropriate equipment under the leadership of an experienced guide.

Riverwalking activity providers in Ireland:

Kilfinane OEC
Outdoor Education Centre
Kilfinane OEC, Kilfinane,
Co. Limerick
Phone: + 353 (0)63 91161/91059
Email: info@kilfinaneoec.com
Web: www.kilfinaneoec.com

Birr OEC
Outdoor Education
Centre   Birr Outdoor Education Centre,
Roscrea Road,
Birr, Co. Offally
Phone: + 353 (0)509 20029
Email: birr@oec.ie
Web: www.oec.ie/birr

Gartan OEC
Outdoor Education Centre
Church Hill, Letterkenny,
Donegal Phone: +353(0)749137032
Email: office@gartan.com
Web: www.gartan.com

Petersburg OEC
Outdoor Education Centre

Petersburg Outdoor
Education Centre,
Clonbur,Co. Galway
Phone: +353 (0) 94 954 6483
Email: info@petersburg.ie
Web: www.petersburg.ie

Killary Adventure Centre
Adventure Centre
Killary Adventure Company,
Leenane, Co. Galway
Phone: + 353 (0)95 43411
Web: www.killaryadventure.ie

Delphi Advenure Co.
Adventure Centre Leenane,
Connemara,
Co. Galway
Phone: +353 (0)95 42208
Email: info@delphiadventure.com
Web: www.delphiadventureholidays.ie

The Táin Adventure Centre
Adventure Centre
Omeath,Co. Louth
Phone: +353 (0)42 937 5385
Email: tainhol@eircom.net
Web: www.tainadventure.net

The Bluelough Mountain and
Water Sports Centre
The Corncrane building, Lower square, Castlewellan,
Co. Down BT31 9DQ
Ph: +44 (0)28 4377 0714

Email: info@mountainandwaater.com
Web: www.mountainandwater.com

Adventure Centre
Lilliput House, Lough Ennell, Co.
Westmeath.
Phone: +353 (0)44 9226789
Email: lilliputadventure@eircom.net
Web: www.lilliputadventure.com

Activity Centre
98 Bryansford Road,
Newcastle, Co Down BT33 0LF
Phone: +44(0)28 4372 3933
Email: Dublin@pd-group.eu
Web: www.pd-group.eu

Activity Centre
62 Main Street, Gortin,BT79 8NH
Phone: +44 (0)28 8164 8346
Email: info@gortin.net
Web: www.gortin.net

Accommodation:

The Kilfinane Outdoor Education Centre provides ensuite rooms, twin rooms and camping facilities to groups enrolled on one of their activities. B&Bs in Kilfinane include Woodview B&B (+353 (0)63 91106, Glebe Road, Kilfinane), St Andrews Villa (+353 (0)63 91008, Kilfinane) and Lantern Lodge (+353 (0)63 91085, Ballyorgan, Kilfinane). For a list of accommodation options in the Ballyhoura area check out the accommodation section on www.ballyhouracountry.com or contact the Kilfinane tourist office at + 353 (0)63 91300.

Other attractions:

Hill walking is popular in and around Ballyhoura. The Ballyhoura International walking festival takes place every May with organised walks on one of the twenty routes in the area, including the Ballyhoura Way.

The Beast of Ballyhoura adventure race (www.ballyhourabeast.com), which takes place in August and runs continuously over twenty-two to twenty-eight hours, involves mountain biking, orienteering, mountaineering, abseiling, kayaking and shooting.

The recently opened Ballyhoura mountain biking trail offers three world-class trails, covering 91 km in total, of way-marked routes using a combination of forest roads and newly built single-track trails (see chapter: Mountain biking – Ballyhoura, Limerick).

Best time to go/season:

After heavy rain anytime of the year.

Links:

www.kilfinaneoec.com;
www.ballyhouracountry.com;
www.visitlimerick.com;
www.ballyhoura.com;
www.discoverireland.com;
www.mountaineering.ie.

HORSE TREKKING
ACHILL, CO. MAYO

One of the best ways to see rural Ireland is while trekking on the back of a horse. Ireland offers a diversity of trekking possibilities, from remote mountain trails, through green open valleys or over long sandy beaches. Horse riding is an integral part of Irish culture with Irish-bred horses and jockeys competing for top honours in all equestrian events. Whether you are looking for a gentle trek through the Irish countryside or a gallop along a remote beach, the large number of equestrian centres spread throughout Ireland provide excellent horses and treks to suit all riders.

I arrived at Calveys Equestrian Centre on Achill Island on a beautiful summer's day. Having only had lessons twice in the past, Martina, one of the owners, confirmed that I was a beginner; this unfortunately meant I didn't have enough experience to take the popular beach trek. Riders need galloping experience as horses can be very excitable and at times over-enthusiastic on the beach. I signed up for a short trek over bogland to the inland lake. Not quite the magical fantasy ride I had conjured up in my mind.

Kitted out in a luminous yellow vest and riding helmet, Martina introduced me to my horse, Blaze, the mother of the stables. Our instructors led two Italian children, the horses and myself to the riding pen where, with some guidance, I mounted Blaze. We were then given a crash course in starting, stopping and steering. Satisfied with our performance in the pen, Martina released us onto the quiet country road beside the centre.

The roads on Achill are rarely busy, which gave us the opportunity to trot part of the way down to the lake. It's a little disconcerting to see the world from this elevated and unprotected position; as a beginner you feel at the mercy of this beautiful yet enormous animal. The slow rhythm which you develop as you ride is hypnotising, and after a time you don't have to think too much about the horse. You

can soak up the fresh air and sunshine while getting a whole new perspective on the countryside. Under the guidance of our instructors we trekked down a narrow side road, across a shallow stream and over marsh bogland along the shores of the small lake that overlooks the impressive Minaun cliffs. Blaze was very surefooted and was clearly very familiar with the route, which was exactly the kind of reassurance a beginner like me needed. The lake was busy with people taking windsurfing lessons. After a short ride along the bank of the lake we swung around and trekked back along the same route to the stables.

The next morning I awoke early to get a glimpse of the riders galloping along the beach. A few more lessons and I should be ready to join them. Whether you're new to horse riding or an experienced rider, Achill has a trek to suit all levels. From gentle trots through mountain bog landscape to exciting gallops along Keel strand, they all offer a little bit of magic.

Getting there:

Calveys Equestrian Centre is located half way between Keel and the 'deserted village' on Achill Island. On entering Keel take a right turn after the Minaun View bar. Continue for about 400 metres before taking a left turn signposted Achill IT Centre, then take the first right turn on this road. The Equestrian Centre is located at the end of this narrow road. Westport has the nearest train station (www.irishrail.ie) and is also well served by bus (www.buseireann.ie). Daily bus services Keel to Westport, Castlebar and Galway.

The area:

Achill offers an abundance of horse trekking opportunities, along miles of sandy beaches, mountain tracks, natural bog trails or through the deserted famine village.

Provider:

Calvey's Equestrian Centre has a wide range of treks that make the most of the spectacular Achill scenery. These include one, two, three and four-hour treks, full and half-day tours, weekend tours and five-day packages.

All treks are supervised by knowledgeable, helpful and friendly guides. There is also instruction and tuition for beginners and improvers with experienced instructors.

Calveys Equestrian Centre, Keel, Achill, Co Mayo (yevlacm@hotmail.com, +353 (0)98 43158).

More about Horse Trekking

The Association of Irish Riding Establishments regulates standards at riding schools and equestrian centres in Ireland. For a list of approved riding schools throughout Ireland see their website (+353 (0)1 281 0963, www.aire.ie).

Accommodation:

Achill is popular during the summer months, so book accommodation in advance of travelling. The equestrian centre is located outside the village of Keel.

Hostels: The Railway hostel, Achill Sound (+353 (0)98 45187), Valley House holiday hostel and bar (www.valley-house.com, +353

(0)98 47204). Camping: Keel Sandybanks caravan and camping park (www.achillcamping.com, +353 (0)98 43211), Lavelle's Golden Strand caravan and camping park, Dugort (+353 (0)98 47232), Seal Caves camping and caravan park, Dugort (+353 (0)98 43262). B&Bs near the equestrian centre include Achill Isle House (+353 (0)98 43355), Atlantic Breeze (+353(0)98 43189), Fuchsia Lodgen (+353 (0)98 43350), Joyce's Marian Villa(+353 (0)98 43111), Roskeel House (+353 (0)98 45272), Stella Maris(+353 (0)98 43297, www.stellamarisachill.com). Hotels: Achill Cliff House hotel (www.achillcliff.com, +353 (0)98 43400), Achill Head hotel (+353 (0)98 43108). For a full list of accommodation options on Achill Island contact the Achill Island tourist office (www.achilltourism.com, +353 (0)98 47353), open all year round.

Other attractions:

Not to be missed is the Atlantic drive, a 40-km trip around the entire island that includes an impressive view of Keel strand and Clare Island from the top of Minaun (466 metres). The deserted village is an impressive reminder of days gone. The eighty stone cottages located at the foot of the majestic Slievemore mountain are remnants of a nomadic people who moved between coastal and inland settlements during the 1800s.

The narrow quiet roads are perfect for cycling. Bikes can be rented from O'Malley's Island Sports (+353 (0)98 43125) in Keel. Other activites on the island include windsurfing (www.windwise.ie, +353 (0)98 43958), scuba diving (www.achilldivecentre.com, +353 (0)87 234 9884), deep sea angling (Tom Burke, +353 (0)98 47257), surfing (www.achill-surf.com, Shane Cannon, +353 (0)86 228 8566), sea kayaking (Tomás Mac Lochlainn organises sea kayaking safaris and rents surfboards on Keel strand +353 (0)98 45085), golf at the nine-hole course in Keel (watch out for the sheep) (+353 (0)98 43456). There are plenty of hill walking possibilities (see chapter: Hill Walking – Achill Head, Co Mayo).

McDowell's Hotel and Activity Centre offers a range of activities including sailing, surfing and canoeing courses (www.achill-leisure.ie, +353 (0)98 43148).

A traditional Irish music festival, Scoil Acla festival, takes place in the first two weeks of August, from July to September the Achill Yawl festival and in March a hill walking festival. See www.achilltourism.com for more information.

Best time to go/season:

Anytime from May to September.

Links:

www.achilltourism.com
www.visitachill.com
www.achill247.com
www.aire.ie (Association of Irish Riding Establishments).

HILL WALKING
ACHILL HEAD, CO. MAYO

It was a mid-summer's evening and the warm sun had cast a shadow over the deserted Keem bay. Starting from the information sign in the lower car park we made our way up the steep grassy bank. A short but demanding climb along a well-trodden path took us to the cliff top. From here we had a spectacular panorama of Croaghaun to the north, the Slievemore to the northeast and the impressive Minaun cliffs to the southeast.

A former coastguard watchtower is located on Moyteoga head on the southern tip of the cliff ridge. The watchtower was once used to monitor warship activity off the coast. If you are extremely lucky you may be able to spot basking sharks, the world's second largest fish, from the tower. In the mid-1940s Achill Basking Shark Fisheries operated from Keem

bay. The sharks were trapped in nets attached to the cliffs and killed by harpoon from currachs (traditional Island boats). The sharks were then towed by larger boats to Purteen harbour further east, where the valuable oil was extracted from the liver. After the initial success of the 1940s and 1950s the numbers of sharks declined due to over-fishing. In the 1970s fishing for basking sharks ceased.

With no basking sharks to be seen we followed the cliff edge northwestwards towards Achill head. There is open grazing on Achill and as a result there are sheep everywhere. The cliffs were no exception; a couple of sheep seemed to pose for the camera in very precarious positions. From one of the higher peaks along the cliff we got our first view of Achill head, which is shaped like the tail of a dinosaur, gently sloping into the water with the tail end protruding out of the water.

Down in the valley the remnants of Bunowna booley village can be seen, a ruined settlement of seventeen houses, nine of which are visible. The settlement was used as a summer residence for young herders who brought their animals here for summer pasture. Looking out to sea we also had a clear view across to Clare Island.

the Atlantic ocean, a red glow illuminating the high cliff face. The sun was almost down and the midges (small biting flies) had almost devoured us when we packed up and began walking to the car park. We took a lower path back to Keem bay, avoiding the ups and downs along the cliff edge, passing along the way the ruins of Charles Boycott's house.

Boycott, a landlord who first came to Achill

At the final knoll we sat and admired what is probably the best view you can get of the Croaghaun cliffs. The northeast face of the mountain falls away dramatically almost from its peak down to sea level. These cliffs are said to be the highest in Europe. The northeast face of Croaghaun is also home to the highest corrie lake in Ireland, Bunnafreva lough west, which sits at over 1,000 ft above sea level. The lake, however, cannot be seen from Achill head. We sat and watched the sun set over

around 1857, leased land at Keem bay and built a house and other buildings. After this residence was burned down he moved to Corrymore House, leasing 70,000 acres of land around Lough Acorrymore. Under the Irish National Land league formed by Michael Davitt in 1879, local tenants were urged not to pay the unfair rents or to work for Boycott. It was thus that his name became part of the English language with the word 'boycott' meaning 'to shun'.

There are many hill walking possibilities

on Achill Island, the Achill head walk is one of the easiest and yet most rewarding of all. You won't be disappointed.

Getting there:

Achill Island is located on the west coast of Co. Mayo in the northwest of Ireland. The island is connected to the mainland by a bridge and is only accessible by road. Achill is 295 km from

Dublin (N5), 230 km from Shannon airport, and 350 km from Belfast. For detailed road directions see www.achilltourism.com/directions.html. Knock airport (www.knockairport.com) is 110 km from Achill and is the nearest airport. Knock offers flights to several British destinations and a limited number of trans-Atlantic routes.. Westport has the nearest train station (www.irishrail.ie) and is also well served by bus (www.buseireann.ie). Daily bus services connect Dooagh to Westport, Castlebar and Galway. This

round-trip walk begins and ends at the lower car park beside Keem strand on the western tip of Achill Island about 2km from Dooagh.

The area:

Achill is the largest island off the coast of Ireland. Measuring 20 kms from east to west and 18 km from north to south, the island enjoys a coastline of about 120 km and supports a community of about 3,500 people. There are currently five blue flag beaches on the island.

The dramatic cliffs of Croaghaun (668 metres) are said to be the highest sea cliffs in Europe, although the people of Slieve League in Donegal controversially disagree. The remote cliffs are inaccessible by road and are home to some rare birdlife, including the protected species, chough, and the peregrine falcon.

More about Hill Walking:

The walk takes around 2.5 hours. After the initial ascent to a height of 198 metres, the rest of the walk is easy with small undulating hills taking you along the cliff edge, giving spectacular views out to the tip of Achill head. Generally the going is good; well grazed grass allows for easy walking conditions. There are patches of marshy land that can be avoided for the most part. This walk follows the cliff edge and shouldn't be attempted in poor conditions; wear good walking boots and bring insect repellent to fight off the biting midges. It's possible to climb out to the tip of Achill head but this should only be attempted by experienced climbers using climbing equipment. If you are feeling energetic you can include climbing Mt Croaghaun (668 metres) or Mt Slievemore (672 metres). There are plenty of hill-walking routes on Achill; a guidebook available from Achill tourisim details fourteen circular walks.

For more information about hill walking in Ireland and a comprehensive list of hill walking clubs; contact the Mountaineering Council of Ireland at (+353 (0)1 625 1115) or check out their website www.mountaineering.ie.

Accommodation:

Achill is popular during the summer months, so book accommodation in advance of travelling. The nearest town to the cliff walk is Dooagh.

Hostels:

The Railway hostel, Achill Sound (+353 (0)98 45187), Valley House holiday hostel and bar (www.valley-house.com, +353 (0)98 47204). Camping: Keel Sandybanks caravan and camping park (www.achillcamping.com, +353 (0)98 43211), Lavelle's Golden Strand caravan and camping park, Dugort (+353 (0)98 47232), Seal Caves camping and caravan park, Dugort (+353 (0)98 43262). B&Bs near the cliffs include New Verona House, Dooagh (+353 (0)98 43160), Réalt na Mara (+353 (0)98 43005), Teach Cruachán (+353 (0)98 43301), West Coast House, Dooagh (+353 (0)98 43317). Hotels: Achill Cliff House hotel (www.achillcliff.com, +353 (0)98 43400), Achill Head hotel (+353 (0)98 43108). For a full list of accommodation options on Achill Island contact the Achill Island tourist office (www.achilltourism.com, +353 (0)98 47353), open all year round.

Other attractions:

Not to be missed is the Atlantic drive, a 40-km trip around the entire Island that includes an impressive view of Keel strand and Clare Island from the top of Minaun (466 metres). The deserted village is an impressive reminder of days gone. The eighty stone cottages located at the foot of the majestic Slievemore mountain are remnants of a nomadic people who moved between coastal and inland settlements during the 1800s.

The narrow quiet roads are perfect for cycling, and in 2008 several routes are due

Map labels:
- Achill Head
- (256 m)
- Bunawana
- Booley Village
- Croaghaun (644m)
- Boycotts House
- Keem Strand
- Moyteoge Head (198m)

to be way marked. Bikes can be rented from O'Malley's Island Sports (+353 (0)98 43125 in Keel. Other activites on the island include windsurfing (www.windwise.ie, +353 (0)98 43958), scuba diving (www.achilldivecentre. com, +353 (0)87 234 9884), deep sea angling (Tom Burke, +353 (0)98 47257), surfing (www.achill-surf.com, Shane Cannon, +353 (0)86 228 8566), sea kayaking (Tomás Mac Lochlainn organises sea kayaking safaris and rents surfboards on Keel strand +353 (0)98 45085), golf at the nine-hole course in Keel (watch out for the sheep) (+353 (0)98 43456) and horse riding (Calveys Equestrian Centre, +353 (0)98 43158). See chapter: Horse Trekking, Ahill, Co. Mayo.

McDowell's Hotel and Activity Centre offers a range of activities including sailing, surfing and canoeing courses (www.achill-leisure.ie, +353 (0)98 43148).

A traditional Irish music festival, Scoil Acla festival, takes place in the first two weeks of August, from July to September the Achill Yawl festival and in March a hill walking festival. See www.achilltourism.com for more information.

Best time to go/season:
May to early September. You must have good weather for this trip since the route passes along the edge of towering cliffs.

Links:
www.achilltourism.com
www.visitachill.com
www.achill247.com
www.mountainviews.ie

SAILING LOUGH REE, ATHLONE, CO. ROSCOMMON

We arrived on a crisp December morning at the Hodson Bay hotel in Athlone. Our instructor, Phil Knowd, from the Irish sailing academy was waiting at the car park overlooking Lough Ree. We had booked the three-hour 'taste of sailing' course, the first certified sailing course available on a national sailing syllabus. The Irish Sailing Association (ISA) has implemented a small boat sailing scheme used by all ISA certified instructors. The scheme outlines safety standards and a progressive list of sailing courses designed to take students from sailing beginner up to expert sailor. The aim of the 'taste of sailing' course is to offer a brief but positive experience of the thrill of sailing small boats. After quick introductions we helped Phil launch the 21-foot keelboat. In the first half an hour Phil, aided by a white board, took us through the basic principles of sailing.

Sailing involves a lot of terms that describe specific actions or pieces of equipment. Phil began by familiarising us with all the equipment on the boat and important terms used in sailing. Both of us had been on sailboats several times; however, we had always been told where to go, what to pull and when to pull it. The business of knowing what the equipment was called and what it was for was completely alien to us. The front of a boat is called the bow, the rear is the stern, the left side is the port and the right the starboard. The two sails on the boat are called the main sail and the jib (front sail). Lines that raise sails are called halyards, while those that take them down are called downhauls or cunninghams. The boom is attached to the mainsail and is to be avoided when tacking (turning into the wind), as it swings overhead to the opposite side of the boat. A sailing boat is turned by a rudder, which itself is controlled by a tiller or a wheel, while at the same time trimming (adjusting) the sheets (lines that adjust the sails). There was a lot to learn.

Phil explained the different 'points of sail', the sailing boat's course in relation to the wind direction. When the boat is travelling approximately perpendicular to the wind, this is called reaching. For most modern sailboats, reaching is the fastest way to travel. The wind, or 'no go zone', is about 45° either side of the true wind. If you turn the boat directly into the wind (no go zone) and trim the sheets you can bring the boat to a complete stop.

Phil assured us that we wouldn't remember all the terms in one lesson (he was right)

but with practice the names and terms would become second nature. When it was time to put the theory into practice we cast off and used the small onboard motor to take us out of the marina. During our lesson, one person had responsibility to man the jib sheets, the other to control the rudder and the main sail sheets. The three-hour lesson flew by as we each took turns mastering the different jobs on the boat. We sailed in a figure of eight formation, practising tacking (turning) into the wind and bringing the boat to a complete stop.

To finish off we needed to sail against the wind to bring the boat back to the marina. Sailing against the wind involves moving in a zig-zag formation, gaining ground on each turn. While trying to put our new skills into practice was a little more taxing than our previous sailing trips, it was great to finally have some understanding of what we were doing on the boat.

Depending on the conditions and your desire for speed, sailing can be either an exhilarating adrenaline rush or an easy relaxing cruise on quiet waters. Whatever your preference, sailing offers something for everyone. Ireland has plenty of sailing schools and safe places to learn to sail. If you're interested in learning, book a course with one of the many sailing instructors around the country.

Getting there:
The launching point is located at Hodson Bay, Lough Ree, Athlone. Hodson Bay is located infront of the Hodson bay hotel. Athlone is 126 km from Dublin, 93 km from Galway, 227 km

from Belfast, 219 km from Cork and 134 km from Shannon.

Driving: From Dublin take the N6 (main Dublin to Galway road), on the Athlone town bypass take the Roscommon exit (N61). Follow the road for about 5 kms. Hodson bay is well signposted, and is located on the right. Daily train (www.irishrail.ie) and bus services (www.buseireann.ie) serve Athlone. The Athlone train station is located 5 km from Hodson Bay.

The area:

Lough Ree is located in the midlands and is the second largest of the three lakes on the river Shannon. It is a large rich limestone lake of 10,500 hectares stretching for about 25 km from Lanesborough in the north to Athlone in the south. The lake is about 7 km wide at its widest point.

Provider:

The Irish Sailing Academy (www.irishsailingacademy.com, +353 (0)49 952 9750) are certified Irish Sailing Association (ISA) instructors.

The Irish Sailing Academy offer courses in three different locations around Ireland

o   Malahide Marina Centre, Dublin
o   Hodson bay, Athlone
o   Rosmoney, Mayo

A newly opened sailing centre located at Hodson bay in Athlone will offer a range of sailing and powerboat courses on Lough Ree.

Course Prices

Duration	Price
3 hours	€140
1 day	€200
2 days	€290
5 days / 2 weekends	€550

More about sailing:

The Irish Sailing Association (ISA) is the national governing body for sailing in Ireland. The ISA small boat sailing scheme can be completed in a boat of your choice (catamaran, small keelboat or sailing dinghy). Course duration depends on how quickly you grasp the techniques and at what level you are at. Typically a Level 1 course can be completed in a three-hour lesson while more advanced levels can take several days to master. For a comprehensive list of sailing clubs and activity providers check out the club listings on the Irish Sailing Association website www.sailing.ie.

Accommodation:

There are numerous hotels in Athlone, including the Athlone Springs hotel (www.athlonespringshotel.com, +353(0)90 649 0711), Radisson SAS hotel (www.radissonsas.com, +353 (0)90 644 2655), Creggen Court hotel (www.creggancourt.com, +353 (0)90 647 7777) and the Hodson Bay hotel overlooking Lough Ree (www.hodsonbayhotel.com, +353 (0)90 648 0500). Rates range from €90 to €185 per person, depending on the room type and time of year. The Hodson Bay caravan park (+353 (0)90 649 2448), open from 1 June to

31 August, offers camping and caravan facilities on the shores of Lough Ree. B&Bs in the area include Reeside B&B (+353 (0)90 649 2051, Barrymore, Athlone), St Ruth's farmhouse (www.struths.com, +353 (0)90 648 8090) and Dalys tavern, located within the town (www.dalystavern.ie,+353 (0)90 648 9082). For more accommodation options see www.athlone.ie or contact the Athlone tourist office (seasonal) on + 353 (0)90 649 4630.

Other attractions:

Athlone's position on the river Shannon at the foot of Lough Ree provides the ideal location for water and leisure enthusiasts. Guided boat trips of Lough Ree, river cruises and fishing are popular water activities along the Shannon. Clubs and activity providers in the area include Athlone Boat Club, Athlone Triathlon Club (www.triathlone.com), Lough Ree Yacht Club (www.lryc.ie), Lough Ree Power Boat School (www.powerboat.org) and the Athlone Equestrian Centre (+353 (0)86 243 3609). Athlone has a range of golf clubs to choose from: Athlone Golf Club, the Christy O' Connor-designed championship golf course at Glasson Golf & Country Club and the traditional championship golf course of Mount Temple Golf Club. The Inland Waterways Association has outlined several walks around Lough Ree (walks.iwai.ie/ree/index.shtm).

Athlone and district offers a wide variety of attractions and historical sites including Athlone castle and the Clonmacnoise monastic site. The large ecclesiastical site boasts three high crosses, a cathedral, seven churches and two round towers and was once an important centre of religion, learning, trade, craftsmanship and politics. Guided daily tours are available. (www.heritageireland.com, +353 (0)90 967 4195).

Best time to go/season:
Courses offered all year.

Links:
www.sailing.ie(Irish Sailing Association), www.iwai.ie;
www.athlone.ie (Athlone tourist information), www.iws.ie (Irish Water Safety).

HIGH ROPES COURSE
KILLARY ADVENTURE CENTRE,
LEENANE, CO. GALWAY

Ropes courses are fast becoming the most popular activities at adventure centres around the world. The combination of vertical and horizontal challenges involves climbing wooden poles, traversing cables, monkey rings and ropes strung between high wooden platforms or trees.

We arrived in Leenane after a night of torrential rain and gale force winds. I met with our guide, Henry, at the Killary Adventure Centre located just outside Leenane beside Ireland's only fjord. The wind had died down considerably but there was still a deluge of rain. Henry assured us that the conditions would only add to the enjoyment. There were a total of ten people, three different groups, consisting of three women and seven men. Each person in the group was given a climbing harness and a helmet. After a safety talk and equipment demonstration we were led out to the first of three challenges.

The first challenge involved a lot of teamwork; four people had to climb a 6-metre-high telegraph pole one after the other. All four climbers had to stand together on top of the pole on a small platform that realistically could only hold two people. I think each of us was a little nervous but put on a brave face. Four other people in the group had the job of belaying the climbers from the ground. Belaying involves removing the slack from a safety rope attached to the climber as they ascend. If the climber falls, then they will freefall the distance of the slack or unprotected rope before the safety rope catches them. I wasn't nervous about the challenge but about the fact that I was placing my life in the hands of a guy called Dave from Offaly whom I had only met five minutes beforehand. Dave had little sympathy: 'If you can't trust an Offaly man with your life who can you trust?' Who indeed? I was the first person up from my group of four climbers. My job was relatively easy since the platform was completely free once I reached the top. The next two climbers managed to make it onto the platform with guidance from our guide on foot and hand placement. We stood in a tight embrace about 6 metres above the ground on the rocking pole as the fourth climber made his way to the top. To get the last climber up onto the platform required a lot of team work, each person giving a helping hand and giving away vital foot space to the last climber. With all four on top we received a deserved round of applause from below. As a finale we had to stretch out our hands and, taking the hand of the person beside us, we leaned back and created a star shape on the top of the pole. This was nerve racking, leaning back over the edge of a 6 metre pole with strangers (one from Offaly) keeping you up. It wasn't long before the star collapsed and the safety ropes were called into action.

The next challenge was called 'leap of faith', and involved two people climbing up an even higher telegraph pole. Both had to jump simultaneously from the top of the pole to a trapeze pole positioned about 6 feet from the jumping position. We took turns climbing to the top; the first pair managed to catch the trapeze pole easily so Henry decided to position it a little further out. The next two missed the target, resulting in a gut-wrenching fall, with relief registering on their faces as the safety ropes kicked in and took their weight. When it came to our turn the wind picked up and it began to rain heavily. There was no point stopping now. I was paired off with my friend Lee who is 1 foot shorter than me, which put us at a bit of a disadvantage since to reach the trapeze pole both people must grab it at the same time otherwise the first person will swing it out of reach of the second. Lee climbed up first and stood ready on the top. I climbed to the top but found it hard to stand on the small platform. Henry directed me to foot holds and I was soon standing side by side with Lee. We were both trying not to look down and concentrating on the trapeze pole ahead of us. As Henry counted down

from three I realised it looked just beyond our reach. Lee jumped a split second before me, and we reached the trapeze pole at the same time. We made it.

After a quick break for tea and biscuits we set into the last challenge – Ireland's highest outdoor climbing wall. With three graded climbs from easy to difficult, each climber could choose the difficulty level they were comfortable with. Our arms were burning by the end of the session.

The ropes course pushes participants to their own perceived limits, teaches them about risk taking and performing under pressure and forces them to work as a team to complete the task. If you are looking for an adrenaline-packed challenge give the ropes course a try.

Getting there:

Killary Adventure Centre is located 5.5 km west of Leenane village in Co. Galway. Leenane is about halfway between Clifden and Westport on the N59.

If you are driving from Galway follow the signs for the N59 to Clifden and after passing through the villages of Moycullen and Oughterard you will arrive at Maam Cross (Peacock's hotel will be on your right). At this crossroads turn right, following signs for 'Leenaun'. At the next T-junction at Cians pub, turn left. This road will bring you into the village of Leenane. Keep left and after another 5 km, with Killary harbour on your right, you will see the sign for Killary Adventure/K2. If driving from Dublin, take the N5 to Westport (its about thirty minutes shorter than driving via Galway). From Westport follow the signs for Leenane along the N59. Once in Leenane take a right over the bridge and follow the road for 5 km; the centre is on the left hand side.

If travelling by public transport, take a train (www.irishrail.ie) to Galway or Westport and a bus (www.buseireann.ie) from there. A daily bus runs from Galway city to the Sleepzone hostel in Killary. It is called the Sleepzone bus and leaves from outside the Sleepzone hostel just off Eyre Square. Contact the adventure centre for more details.

The area:

Killary Adventure Centre is located on the southern shores of Ireland's only fjord at Killary harbour. The fjord forms a partial border between counties Galway and Mayo. It is 16 km long and in the centre it is over 45 metres deep. The Mweelrea mountain range, at 817 metres, the highest mountains in Connemara, dominates the northern shore. The beautiful village of Leenane was made famous by its appearance in the film *The Field* in 1989 staring Richard Harris, John Hurt and Tom Berenger.

Provider:

Killary Adventure Centre offers adventure activities to cater for all ages and levels of fitness. Activities include kayaking, rock climbing, abseiling, sailing, gorge walking, hill walking, archery, clay pigeon shooting, windsurfing, laser combat, wakeboarding, orienteering and the high ropes challenge. A three-hour session on the ropes course costs €45 for adults and €28 for children. A day of activity (10am – 5pm) costs €80 for adults and €45 for kids.

Prices for the different activities depend on the group size, accommodation options and the activities you choose. For a full list of packages and prices check out the Killary website, www.killaryadventure.com.

More about High Ropes courses:

The high ropes course activity is relatively new to Ireland, the following list displays current adventure centres offering high ropes course activities.

Killary Adventure Co.

Adventure Centre Company
Leenane, Co. Galway
Phone: +353 (0)95 43411/42276
Email: adventure@killary.com
Web: www.killaryadventure.ie

Kippure Estate Lodge

Kippure EstateManor, Kilbride,Blessington,
Co. Wicklow
Phone: +353 (0)1 458 2889
Email: info@kippure.com
Web: www.kippure.com

Delphi Advenure Co.

Adventure Centre
Leenane,Connemara,
Co. Galway
Phone: +353 (0)95 42208
Email: info@delphiadventure.com
Web: www.delphiadventureholidays.ie

Ireland Xtreme Activity Provider

Collinstown Business Park, Air-
port Rd, Cloghran, Co. Dublin
Phone: +353 (0)1 8622000
Email: info@irelandxtreme.ie
Web: www.irelandxtreme.ie

Donegal Adventure Centre

Adventure Centre
Bayview Ave,
Bundoran, Co. Donegal
Phone: +353 (0)7 1984 2418
Email: info@donegaladventurecentre.net

Web: www.donegaladventurecentre.net

Carlingford Adventure Centre

Adventure Centre
Tholsel St., Carlingford, Co. Louth
Phone: + 353 (0)42 9373 100
Email: info@carlingfordadventure.com
Web: www.carlingfordadventure.com

University of Limerick Activity Centre

Adventure Centre
Two Mile Gate,Killaloe, Co. Clare.
Phone: +353 61 376622
Email: info@ulac.ie
Web: www.ulac.ie

Lurgaboy Lodge

Adventure Centre
12 Gosford Road,Armagh BT60 1LQ
Phone: +44 (0) 28 3755 2425
Email: info@lurgaboylodge.com
Web: www.lurgaboylodge.com

Accommodation:

Killary Adventure Centre (K2) (www.killary.
com, +353 (0)95 43411/42276) has accommodation for groups and individuals coming to
Killary to take part in adventure activities. The
K2 can cater for large groups of up to eighty
in a combination of double, twin and dorm
room accommodation (six and four-bed dorm
rooms). Prices range from €18 to €24 for
dorm beds (from four to six-bed dorms) and
€25 to €32 for twin/double rooms. Contact
K2 to find out about their adventure packages,

which include accommodation and a range of activities.

Sleepzone hostel (www.sleepzone.com, +353 (0)95 42929 or +353 (0)91 566999) offers both private and dormitory accommodation (all ensuite). There is free internet and WiFi access, a bureau de change, tourist information, self-catering kitchen, residents' bar, cable TV, bike hire and tennis courts. Rates vary from between €13 and €22 for a dorm bed (from three to ten-bed dorms) and between €22 and €40 for a twin/single room.

The 200-year-old Leenane hotel (www.leenanehotel.com, +353 (0)95 42249) is open from 28 March to 18 November and offers bed and breakfast at between €55 and €69 pps depending on the season.

Other attractions:

There are plenty of activities to keep you busy in the area.

o Drive the Connemara loop (www.goconnemara.com).
o Swim at Lettergesh, Glassilaun or one of the many other blue flag beaches on the Renvyle peninsula and throughout Connemara.
o Hike one of the many nearby mountain ranges: the Twelve Bens, Mweelrea, the Maumturk mountains or Croagh Patrick (see chapter: Hill Walking – Croagh Patrick, Co. Mayo) or from Lennane hike to Asleigh Fall (4 km from Leenane on the Westport road).

o Take a cruise on the fjord (www.killary-cruises.com).
o Both Killary (www.killary.com) and Delphi (www.delphiadventure.com) adventure centres offer a range of adventure activities.
o Visit Kylemore Abbey and the Victorian walled garden (www.kylemoreabbey.com).
o Visit the Connemara national park and avail of one of the many guided walks.
o Visit the scenic Inishbofin Island (www.inishbofin.com).
o Bike or hike one of the many nearby trails (www.westirelandcycling.com).
o Scuba dive (www.scubadivewest.com).
o Go fishing (fishing permits can be obtained from Eriff Fisheries in Leenane or from Delphi Lodge).

Best time to go/season:
 Good all year round.

Links:
www.killaryadventure.ie
www.goconnemara.com
www.killarycruises.com

WIND SURFING
RUSHEEN BAY, CO. GALWAY

Windsurfing combines elements of surfing and sailing, and embraces skills common to wakeboarding, water-skiing, snowboarding and skateboarding. Many would argue that it offers more flexibility of movement and more opportunity for creativity than other sail-powered craft. Jumps, loops spins and other freestyle moves can be achieved on a sailboard, and windsurfers were the first to ride the world's largest waves (such as Jaws in Maui). An Irish-born windsurfer, Finian Maynard, even holds the world speed record for a sailing craft – 48.70 knots or 53.88 mph. In windsurfing sailboards or windsurf boards are powered by a single sail; change of direction is achieved by tilting and carving the board while rotating the mast and sail. It has become a hugely popular sport in Ireland with many centres throughout the country providing lessons and equipment hire.

We arrived at the Rusheen bay windsurfing school on a sunny September evening. We booked one hour's tuition and a one-hour practice session. We met with Cathal – the owner – and two instructors, Gavin and Jamie. We suited up and headed for the rack of new learning boards. Jamie explained that the new boards available allow for quicker learning time. 'These new large boards are stable in the water, turn easily in light winds and the light sail can be easily pulled out of the water.' It sounded pretty straightforward. It always does.

Our group comprised three beginners. Jamie pointed out the wind direction and asked us which direction the board should be pointed. After a bit of head scratching we agreed that the wind should be at our back. He then went through the basic techniques.

o Stand on the centre of the board with the sail in the water and your back to the wind.
o Place your feet in the centre of the board, bend forward and pick up the sail line.
o Keeping your balance, pull the sail towards you, placing both hands on the sail mast. When stable in the water place one hand at a time on the sail's boom (hand rail).
o The wind should take hold of the sail and you're off.

Only after all three of us had practised this starting routine on the beach were we ready to hit the water.

We each carried our board and sail until we were up to our knees in the shallow water.

In no time at all the three of us were up on the boards with the wind in our sails. It's easier to grasp the basics using these large stable boards. A large second rudder on the bottom of the board helped stability in the water. After about twenty minutes' practising, criss-crossing the bay and hopping off to turn around, Jamie called us in to teach us how to turn while on the board. He instructed us to take one hand off the boom and hold the sail by the mast. Allowing the sail to drop slightly forward caused the board to automatically swing

around in the wind. We then slowly shifted our feet to the opposite side of the board and when the board was facing the right direction we placed both hands back on the boom and allowed the wind to take the sail.

We took a few practice turns under Jamie's supervision. We found out the hard way that it's all too easy to drift down the bay – easy to get down but hard to get back. Jamie explained how important it is to pick a landmark out on the horizon and try to keep the sail pointing towards it; otherwise you will find yourself walking back. To sail back up the bay we needed to criss-cross the bay, with each cross gaining some distance on the return journey.

As the sun started to go down, the wind died off a bit. I chatted with a more experienced windsurfer out on a practice session. We both appeared to be stuck in the same place; she explained that as the wind speed had died down it was time to change to a larger sail. We slowly managed to sail the boards back to land and exchanged our sails for larger, 5 square metre sails. This sail was heavier and harder to control but it did manage to catch the wind. Jamie left us with an hour to practise all we had learned.

Windsurfing is not a sport for the impatient. It takes practice to master the basic skills and a bit of grunt work at times, but when the wind catches your sail and you take off across the water you'll be glad you made the effort.

Getting there:

Rusheen bay is located just outside Galway city on the coastal road to Spiddal. Galway is well served by both bus (www.buseireann.ie) and train (www.irishrail.ie).

By Car:

From Galway city centre, follow the signs for Salthill. Continue along the coast, passing the promenade and the golf club, where you will come to a T-junction. Turn left for Barna /

Spiddal. After about 300 metres you will see a narrow lane branching off to your left. Rusheen Bay Windsurfing Centre is located at the end of this road.

By Bus:

Take Bus Éireann route 2 (Seacrest/Knocknacarra) from Eyre Square and ask the bus driver to drop you off at the bottom of the Ballymoneen Road. When you disembark you will see the sign for the Rusheen Bay Windsurfing Centre across the main road. Follow the lane down past the sign, to the left, until you get to the school.

The area:

Rusheen bay is five minutes from Galway city; it's a shallow enclosed bay perfect for beginners with calm waters and prevailing cross-onshore winds.

Provider:

The Rusheen Bay Windsurfing Centre is open from the first weekend in April until the last weekend in September. It provides a large range of windsurfing equipment to suit all levels, as well as wetsuits.

Opening Times

April, May and September:
Monday to Friday 5 p.m to 8.30 p.m.
Saturday and Sunday 9.30 a.m. to 6 p.m.

June, July and August:
Monday to Friday 9.30 a.m. to 9.30 p.m.

Saturday and Sunday 9.30 a.m. to 6 p.m.

Windsurfers of all abilities are welcome. Four full-time instructors teach up to level 5.

Price List

o Intro lesson – one hour tuition, one hour practice €50
o Three hours tuition with three hours practice €125
o Advanced programme: five hours rental €95
o Ten-hour rental card €180
o Junior six hours tuition €150

Rusheen Bay Windsurfing
(www.rusheenbay.com, +353 (0)87 260 5702).

More about Windsurfing:

The Irish Windsurfing Association (IWA, www.sailing.ie/windsurf) facilitates and approves windsurfing events (competitions, coaching and recreational) throughout the year.

They have outlined a three stage Go Windsurfing scheme:

o Get Up + Go: Basic skills you need in order to feel confident on a board.
o Go4it: Sessions allow you to develop your basic skills and introduce new ones to help you to enjoy planning (skim the surface of the water) in strongerwinds, counterbalancing in a harness and steering with your feet.
o Go! With Style: These master-class clinics are held for competent windsurfers who

are ready to push out their own boundaries in the more challenging conditions of higher wind and waves.

For more information about windsurfing in Ireland and a comprehensive list of wind surfing clubs and activity providers check out the club listings on www.sailing.ie.

Accommodation:

Galway is very popular all summer but particularly during the week-long Galway races and the preceding Galway arts week festival at the end of July. You should book accommodation well in advance of arriving in the area. For a list of accommodation options check out www.discoverireland.ie/west.aspx, www.galway.net/galwayguide/acc/ or contact the Galway tourist office at +353 (0)91 537700.

Other attractions:

Galway is a tourist haven. Some of the top sites in the area are Kylemore Abbey, a picturesque convent and boarding school run by the Benedictine nuns (www.kylemoreabbey.com) and the Connemara national park. Situated at the foot of the Twelve Bens mountain range, the park is home of the wild Connemara ponies, reputed to be the last survivors of the Spanish Armada. The impressive cliff fortress Dún Aengus can be found on Inishmore, the largest of the Aran Islands. The islands can be reached by ferry from Rossaveal (www.arandirect.com or www.aranlslandsferries.com).

There are numerous activities in the Galway area. Climb the Twelve Bens mountains; cycle the remote Conamara roads; go horse riding a stone's throw from the Rusheen Bay Windsurfing Centre (www.galwayhorseriding.com); take part in one of the many adventure activities offered in Leenane by either the Delphi (www.delphiadventureholidays.ie/) or Killary adventure centres (www.killary.com).

Best time to go/season:

Good all year.

Links:

www.sailing.ie/windsurf (Iris Windsurfing Association)
www.magicseaweed.com
www.met.ie (weather monitor)
www.pol.ac.uk/ntslf/tidalp.html
(tide times and heights).

HILL WALKING
CROAGH PATRICK, CO. MAYO

On our first sighting of the impressive quartzite-peaked mountain, Croagh Patrick, we can see why it has been a place of worship for the last 5,000 years. It stands 762 metres above sea level, towering over the surrounding countryside. We visited on 'Reek Sunday' the last Sunday in July, the day 30,000 people climb the mountain as part of an annual pilgrimage in honour of St Patrick. He is said to have fasted for forty days and forty nights on top of the mountain in 441 AD. The Irish Celts had long climbed the mountain at the end of July to worship their sun god, Lugh (the festival of Lughnasa,1st August). Rather than abolish this tradition, St Patrick instead dedicated the pilgrimage to the Christian God. According to Christian folklore, after the forty days St Patrick threw a bell down the side of the mountain, banishing all the snakes of Ireland.

We arrived at 8.30 in the morning to find lines of cars parked on both sides of the road leading up to the Croagh Patrick Visitor Centre, the starting point for the climb. The road on which the centre is built is known as 'Bóthar na Miasa' (The road of the dishes) – it is reputed that the monks of nearby Murrisk Abbey washed their utensils in the local stream. Luckily we got parking in a field beside the visitor centre. Walking sticks were being sold for €3 outside Campbells pub and religious stalls and pamphlet pushers lined the path from the car park to the statue of St Patrick.

The crowds were unbelievable; a long snake-like queue of people ran all the way to the summit and back down again. Abandoned jackets lined a fence on the way up, no doubt to be collected again by their sweaty owners on their descent. The walking conditions were perfect; the sun was shinning with very few clouds in the sky. Two lady walkers on their way down the mountain offered us their walking sticks; we were glad to have them on the steeper section.

People of all ages were walking the mountain, from eighty-year-old women to children as young as six. In the Irish Christian tradition the pilgrimage is seen as an act of penance for wrongdoing, and many of the pilgrims impressively climb the full 762 metres barefooted over the jagged rocks.

We took a break about three quarters way up before starting into the steepest section of the mountain, where a makeshift shop sold overpriced chocolate bars and refreshments. A large number of mountain rescue workers had gathered there at the landing site for the rescue helicopter. Later that day we discovered that one man was taken off the mountain with a heart condition.

The last section of the mountain was tough going; the steep ascent over loose rocks was difficult enough but we also had to contend with falling rocks from the walkers above us.

We finally reached the cloudy mountaintop where a large number of people had gathered around the church perched on the summit. A priest was saying mass from inside a glass room to the many pilgrims gathered around the church. The clouds passed over the summit quickly and allowed us a breathtaking view over Clew bay, north towards Achill and the Nephin Beg range and south towards the Partry mountains, Sheefery hills, Mweelrea and Connemara.

It is estimated to take two hours to climb to the summit and ninety minutes to return. Although faster, we found the descent was far more challenging than the ascent; rocks gave way readily and it was quite easy to lose your footing. The walking sticks proved invaluable. We took our time navigating the steep section looking for the most stable route. The rest of the descent went quickly, and in no time we reached the statue of St Patrick where we gave our walking sticks to two eager climbers.

On returning to the car we all agreed that there was a real sense of achievement for having climbed the holy mountain on Reek Sunday.

Getting there:
Croagh Patrick is located 8 km from Westport in Co. Mayo. It is approximately 92 km from Galway city and 230 km from Dublin city. The climb starts from the Croagh Patrick Information Centre beside Campbells pub. Westport is well served by bus (www.buseireann.ie), train (www.irishrail.ie) and road (N5) from Dublin. The nearest airport is Knock international airport, providing flights to and from Dublin, Britain and European destinations. Shannon airport (180 km south of Westport) and Dublin airport (230 km east of Westport) provide air access from many worldwide destinations.

The area:
Croagh Patrick is 762 metres high, and on a clear day magnificent views of Clew bay and the surrounding south Mayo countryside are to be had from the summit. The drumlins (small but long hills) in Clew bay were formed from melting glaciers at the end of the last Ice Age. According to tradition there is an island in Clew bay for every day of the year. Clare Island, located at the mouth of Clew bay, is said to be the homeland of the pirate queen, Grace O' Malley. Croagh Patrick is part of a

longer east–west ridge; to the west is the mountain Ben Goram, while across Clew bay the impressive Nephin Beg mountain range and Achill Island can be seen.

Twice a year (18 April and 24 August) the setting sun, instead of setting behind the mountain, appears to 'roll' down the northern slope of the mountain, a phenomenon recorded by pre-Christian worshipers on prehistoric inscriptions found 6.5 km to the east of Croagh Patrick at a stone outcrop called the Boheh stone.

Although mineral explorations of this area have found gold, no mining has taken place on this sacred mountain. However, a recent proposal to open a mine near Louisburg has re-ignited the controversy of the early 1990s when mining companies attempted to open commercial quantity gold mines on the side of Croagh Patrick. I imagine any attempt to mine this mountain would be met with fierce opposition from pilgrims brandishing walking sticks.

More about Hill Walking:

The mountain takes about three and a half hours to climb. The ascent begins from the visitor centre, 'Teach na Miasa', which, if required, provides guided tours, car parking, packed lunches, secure lockers and shower facilities (for a nominal fee). The route from the visitor centre is easy to follow. Loose rocks, particularly on the steeper section near the summit, make for difficult walking conditions. It is advisable to take hiking boots, rain gear and some drinking water. You can pur-

chase climbing sticks from the visitor centre, a big help particularly on the descent.

For more information about hill walking in Ireland and a comprehensive list of hill walking clubs; contact the Mountaineering Council of Ireland at (+353 (0)1 625 1115) or check out their website www.mountaineering.ie.

Accommodation:

Westport is a popular tourist town with many hotels, guest houses and B&Bs. See www.westporttourism.com, www.discoverireland.ie or contact the Westport tourist office (+353 (0)98 25711) for a list of available accommodation. There are also a number of B&B establishments located in close proximity to Croagh Patrick, in Murrisk, Lecanvey and Louisburgh. Parkland caravan and camping park (www.westporthouse.ie, +353 (0)98 27766), located 1 km from the town centre and within the scenic Westport house country park, has good camping and caravan facilities. Advanced booking is recommended, particularly if you are planning to climb Croagh Patrick on Reek Sunday.

Other attractions:

There are plenty of things to see and do in Mayo, the third largest county in Ireland.

Explore some of Clew bay's islands, try your hand at deep sea angling, walk the 170 km Western Way, visit one of the many blue flag beaches around Clew bay, visit the Ceide fields, the site of an ancient stone-age tribe or drive the scenic coastal road around Achill Is-

land. The Westport Woods Hotel & Spa (www.westportwoodshotel.com) offer horse trekking around the foothills of Croagh Patrick and beach treks on Murrisk and Bertra beaches. Horizon Ireland offer adventure packed summer camps for kids (www.horizonireland.com). Delphi and Killary adventure centres offer adventure activites in nearby Leenane (see chapter: High Ropes Course – Killary Adventure Centre, Leenane, Co. Galway). The Gaelforce adventure race, held each year in Westport, promises pure adrenaline-packed adventure (www.gaelforcewest.ie).

Best time to go/season:
A fine summer's day between April and September.

Links:
www.croagh-patrick.com
www.westporttourism.com
www.joycescabs.com
www.knockairport.ie
www.westporthouse.ie/camping.htm.

CAVING
BELCOO,
CO. FERMANAGH

I don't like small spaces, yet, strangely, caving has always appealed to me.

We had arranged to have a guide take us to both a wet and a dry cave for a day of adventure; he assured me that he would not put me in a situation where I wasn't comfortable. That decided, we headed for Belcoo in Co. Fermanagh. Caving is the sport of exploring caves; it involves crawling around in mud, getting wet, often squeezing through small and dark places, sometimes even climbing up and down ropes. Marius Leonard greeted us warmly on an icy January morning. A qualified cave guide, he set about kitting us out immediately. We pulled on thermal layers, fleeces and gloves with warm wool socks. Marius provided rough oversuits and wellingtons, together with helmets fitted with head torches. We packed cameras into waterproof bags and headed for the two dry caves Marius had recommended.

Boho cave was just a short walk off the road through some undergrowth. Our guide led us to an imperceptible opening in the ground that was apparently an entrance. Sensing my panic, he quickly explained that the entrance immediately opened into a spacious cave. I opted to go last. Marius led the way and the other two followed quickly behind; as soon as I lowered myself into the hole I was in the cave and I began to relax. We crawled through the mud and turned on our torches to look at the features around us. The roof of the cave sparkled with silver flecks, a phenomenon called 'cave silver' caused by light reflecting off bacteria. It's amazing to look around in this subterranean world and be right next to cave formations such as stalagmites and stalactites that have taken hundreds of years to form. It's difficult to resist the urge to touch these formations but Marius took the time to explain how damaging human interference can be to these fragile ecosystems. We alternated crawling and walking through sections of the cave, stopping for nuggets of information on the formations around us or about local folklore regarding the caves. Boho cave is a maze

cave that should not be entered without a lo-cal experienced guide. The caves are liable to flood, and adventurers have been caught out in the past. It is easy for even the most ex-perienced caver to get turned around in this cave system. After a December of heavy rain the 'dry' Boho cave was of course not entirely dry, but we decided to brave the cold water to explore the cave further. We questioned the sanity of that decision as the water poured in over the top of our wellingtons – the water reached almost to my waist at one point. As we edged our way on our bellies and elbows through a mud-covered passageway I realised I wasn't feeling as claustrophobic as I had an-ticipated. Marius had us stop, sit and turn off our head torches for two minutes at one point; we just listened to the drops of water hitting the ground and water flowing through other parts of the cave while in complete darkness. It was a total removal from the world around us. The last passageway we negotiated was

narrower than the previous ones although a little higher; the sounds of our oversuits rub-bing against the side walls made me distinctly aware of the size of the space we were in. Just as daylight appeared, signalling a cave opening, Maruis indicated a small porthole-sized opening and asked us each to shine our torches into it as we passed. Once outside, he gave us the option of re-entering the cave and squeezing our bodies through the 10 metre long passageway. I jumped at the op-portunity to photograph the others attempting this feat. Marius led the way; I watched him squeeze through the passageway and began to wonder how my substantially larger brother was going to find the additional space he re-quired. My two companions later described their rebirth as having movement limited to only fingers and toes as everything else was wedged against rock on all sides. They came out buzzing with excitement and dripping in sweat, remarkable given that five minutes previously they had been thigh-high in freezing water. The adrenalin pumping, we set off for the second dry cave.

Coolarkin cave was a Victorian show cave in the past, which explains the convenient steps leading right down to the large opening. A 12-metre waterfall cascades off the land above and falls dramatically over the cave opening. The view from the inside out is even more striking. After three hours of dry caving we were ready to return to the cottages for lunch and to prepare ourselves for the wet cave.

We parked by the roadside and crossed a field to White Father's cave (St Augustine's). We found ourselves entering an underground stream almost immediately. We walked through the cave directly under the main Sligo–Enniskillen road, and progressed slowly through the cave. The flowstone, pillars, stalactites and stalagmites around were a welcome distraction from the icy water penetrating our wetsuits. Marius explained that the water would be at knee height for much of the time, then to our waists, then to chests and finally for two short sections we would swim. Just before the final plunge we allowed the icy water to trickle over that vulnerable neck seal on our wetsuits. We swam through the cave, our torches lighting the water ahead of us until we reached a shallow water opening. We emerged into darkness outside and headed straight for a warm shower. I have six words for anyone considering caving in Ireland. Do it, do it, do it.

Getting there:

The Corralea Activity Centre is located in Belcoo, Co. Fermanagh. Belcoo is 50 km from Sligo airport, 127 km from Derry airport, 178 km from Dublin and 152 km from Belfast.

From Sligo take the N16 (signposted Enniskillen) through Manorhamilton and Blacklion to Belcoo. From Enniskillen take the A4 (signposted Belcoo, Sligo) to Belcoo.

In Belcoo take the B52 (signposted Garrison) and continue for 5 km. The Corralea Activity Centre is on the left. The nearest train station is in Sligo town. Trains leave regularly from Connolly station, Dublin to Sligo town (www.irishrail.ie). From Sligo take a bus to Belcoo; for the latest Sligo–Enniskillen bus timetable or other bus connections to Belcoo see www.buseireann.ie. For bus connections in Northern Ireland see www.translink.co.uk.

The area:

The limestone plateau to the west of Lough Erne in Fermanagh and the Cuilcagh Mountain Park on the borders of County Cavan is punctuated with a vast underground network of caves, rivers and karst features. For information about the different caves in Fermanagh and the rest of Ireland check out www. ukcaves.co.uk.

Provider:

Corralea Activity Centre is a family-run centre comprising six holiday cottages in a beautiful woodland setting on the shores of Lough McNean. The centre offers water- and land-based activities and excellent guest accommodation. Activities include cycling, sea surfing, water trampolining, wind surfing, canoeing, archery, climbing (wall), orienteering and caving. For further information see www.activityireland.com or call +44 (0)28 6638 6123.

You will need to bring warm comfortable clothing, a towel and a complete change of clothes. If you are planning to explore a wet cave bring a bathing suit also.

Corralea will provide all the other caving equipment (helmets, torches, oversuits, wellingtons, gloves and wetsuits for people exploring wet caves).

All staff are qualified and experienced and Corralea Activity Centre has full public liability insurance for this activity.

Prices are from £26 per person for a half day caving with a minimum number of seven or £60 per person for a group of two for half day.

More about Caving

The Speleological Union of Ireland (SUI) is the official body representing the interests of speleologists and sporting cavers in Northern Ireland and the Republic of Ireland. Its website, www.caving.ie, contains all you need to know about caving in Ireland, including important safety tips. Contact the SUI for information about caving clubs/organisations in your area.

Accommodation:

The Corralea Activity Centre offers self-cater-ing cottages with or without activities (www.activityireland.com, +44 (0)28 6638 6123).

B&Bs in the area include: Arch House, Marble Arch Road, Florencecourt (www.archhouse.com, +44 (0)28 6634 8452), Customs House Country Inn, Belcoo (www.customshouseinn.com, +44 (0)28 6638 6285), Corralea Forest Lodge, 154 Lattone Road, Belcoo (+44 (0)28 6638 6325), Bella Vista, Cottage Drive (+44 (0)28 6638 6469), Rockview House, Aghavass, Belcoo (+44 (0)28 6638 6534), Macnean House, Main Street, Blacklion (+353 (0)28 7198 53022), Meadow View, Sandhill, Derrygonnelly (+44 (0)28 6864 1233), Corrigans Shore Guest House, Bellanaleck (+44 (0)28 6634 8572), Abocurragh Farm Guest House, Letterbreen (+44 (0)28 6634 8484).

For camping facilities try Rushin House caravan park located one mile outside Belcoo (www.rushinhousecaravanpark.com, +44 (0)28 6638 6519).

For more accommodation options in Fermanagh see www.findfermanagh.com or contact the Fermanagh tourist office at +44 (0)28 6634 6736.

Other attractions:

The Marble Arch European geopark offer daily tours through a section of the marble arch caves (www.marblearchcave.net). Tours of the caves last approximately seventy-five minutes and are suitable for people of any age of average fitness. There are numerous hill-walking routes in the area; Legnabrocky track takes about six hours and starts at the entrance to the Cullcagh mountain park, taking you to the summit of Cuilcagh mountain. The hikers' trail is a branch of the 500-mile Ulster Way; it takes nine hours and starts at Florencecourt House. The Cullcagh Way is a 33 km long-distance route. For a more relaxed walk try either the Cladagh glen walk, following the path beside the Cladagh river, or the Killykeeghan nature reserve, which has a plesent circular route. For more walking suggestions see www.walkni.com or www.walkireland.ie.

Other activities include the kingfisher cycle trail, a 300 mile mapped and signposted cycling trail (see www.cycletoursireland.com) and fishing on Lough Erne, for which licences and permits can be purchased locally (see www.fermanaghlakelands.com). A number of providers in the area offer a range of different activities: these include Corralea Activity Centre (www.activityireland.com), Lakeland Canoe Centre, Enniskillen (+44 (0)28 6632 4250), Lusty Beg Island Activity Centre (www.lustybegisland.com) and Adventure Tours NI www.adventuretoursni.com. The magnificient Florence Court House and gardens are worth visiting (www.enniskillen.com/florencecourt-house.html). If you're looking for some extreme adventure, try mountain biking and mountain running (www.xtnw.com).

Best time to go/season:

The caves may be flooded after heavy rainfall. Contact the Corralea Activity Centre to check conditions and availability.

Links:

www.caving.ie
www.visitmacnean.com (Lough MacNean area website)
www.blacklion.ie
www.cavantourism.com
www.breifne.ie (Breifne area website)
www.enniskillen.com.

BLOKARTING
NUTTS CORNER,
CO. ANTRIM

Blokarting is a new adventure activity that uses wind-powered lightweight karts to propel you along the beach. A blokart is a small compact three-wheeled mini land-yacht that's very easy to set up and use. A steering arm is used to control direction and a sail similar to those found on small dinghies is used to control your speed. Blokarts have the potential to be very fast; the current blokart speed record clocks in at over 90 km/h.

We arrived at an old disused air track in Nutts Corner on a clear winter's day. I was booked on a half-day session with Pat and Terry of Mectec Blokart. Mectec use the track to give blokarting lessons and allow potential blokart buyers to try before they buy. The majority of blokarting takes place on nearby beaches where turning over on the soft sand tends to be more forgiving on the masts than on the hard runway.

We helped Pat unpack the small bags. The karts fold neatly into 1.2 by .7 metre bags that fit easily into the boot of a car. It took less than ten minutes to assemble both blokarts, attaching the three wheels, the steering wheel and mast to the stainless steel chassis.

Pat gave each of us safety glasses, gloves and a helmet and began the lesson by demonstrating how to safely turn over in the kart. 'The important thing to remember is to keep your arms and legs in the cart; the safety belt will stop you from falling out.' There are no breaks on a blokart to stop you need to turn the blokart directly into the wind.

Pat asked us to sail in a figure of eight between the two cones laid out perpendicular to the wind. With one hand on the steering wheel and the other controlling the sheet rope, we flew across the track, whipping the sail around on the corners. Blokarts can turn instantly as long as you're not going too fast; if you are going at a high speed you need to take more rounded corners. The basic rules of blokarting are: keep right of oncoming blokarts and leave enough room between you and other blokarters or obstacles in case you flip over. There were two of us on the track; like karting, the desire to race the blokarts is intense. Mectec are planning a race series to begin in 2008 where blokarters can test their skills against like-minded speed junkies.

Pat gave us sailing and steering tips as we mastered tacking and jibbing the sail. Like dinghy sailing, a tack into the wind is easier than a jibe with the wind. Unlike the tack, a jibe causes the sail to cross quickly to the new side without any luffing, and in a strong wind this sudden change of wind pressure from

one side of the kart to the other can flip the kart if precautions are not taken. We spent our last hour whizzing around the track practising jibing and tacking and trying to get maximum speed out of our sails and karts.

Blokarting is quickly gaining popularity around the world. This eco-friendly sport only requires wind and an open space to be enjoyed. Ireland's miles of sandy beaches exposed to offshore winds provide the ideal conditions.

Getting there:

Lessons take place on a section of disused airfield adjacent to Nutt's Corner roundabout in Co. Antrim. The entrance is just off the A26 on the Nutts Corner to Moira road. The track is situated 16 km from Belfast city and its ferry port, 37 km from Northern Ireland's other major port of Larne and 166 km from Dublin. Belfast international airport is less than 6 km from the track, and is serviced by many of the low-cost airlines from across the UK and Europe (www.belfastairport.com). For bus and train connections to Nutts Corner see www.translink.co.uk.

The area:

Nutts corner was originally the site of a civil airfield, then a Royal Air Force base and subsequently Northern Irelands main civil airport until the 1960s. Today a small section of the site is used by Northern Ireland Carting Club (NICA), the Ulster Karting Club and Mectec Blokarting.

Provider:

Mectec Blokart are Northern Ireland's blokart dealers and are the only fully qualified BLSA

(British Land and Speed Sail Association) instructors in Northern Ireland.

Mectec offer free fifteen-minute 'come and try' sessions, corporate days and half-day beach or track sessions. A half-day session costs £60 per person. They give lessons throughout the country depending on the numbers of students interested.

Anyone over the age of eight can take part. If you take up blokarting you are encouraged to join the BLSA in Northern Ireland and avail of their group insurance policy.

Contact Pat or Terry on +44 (0)28 9082 5352 for a lesson (info@mectectraining.com).

More about Blokarting:

Blokarts are like sand yachts but smaller and much more portable. First designed in New Zealand by Paul Becket as a recreation product for the entire family, the blokart is controlled using only the hands, meaning that a person's size and mobility are not important factors. Blokarts are also very safe, providing the right protective equipment and precautions are taken. Because of its small size and extreme manoeuvrability the blokart can be used almost anywhere – from beaches to car parks, sports and recreation areas, tennis courts and even on ice, the wheels being replaced with skis and ice skates.

There are three types of blokart: classic, sport and pro. Currently there are very few blokarts in Ireland; new blokarters are encouraged to buy the sports version if they plan to partake in Blokart races. This ensures that all racers have similar kart specifications. A sports blokart costs around £1,500.

Weighing in at only 29 kg the blokart is portable enough to fit in the boot of most cars. It can be assembled from its carry bag in a few minutes with no tools required.

Accommodation:

Nutts Corner is 17 km from Belfast city. For accommodation options in Belfast or the rest of Northern Ireland check out the accommodation section on www.discovernorthernireland.com or call the Northern Ireland tourist office on +44 (0)28 9024 6609. For accommodation near Nutts Corner try Keef Halla B&B, where prices range from £45 to £60 (+44 (0)28 9082 5491, www.keefhalla.com), Caldhame Lodge B&B (+44 (0)28 9442 3313, www.caldhamelodge.co.uk) or Glendona House B&B(+44 (0)28 9442 2283, www.glendona.com).

Other attractions:

Fishing, windsurfing and sailing are popular on nearby Lough Neagh. The northern coast has excellent surfing spots around Portstewart and Portrush. Fairhead in northeast Antrim has hundreds of climbing routes in the mid to upper grades. For more information about outdoor activities in Northern Ireland check out www.outdoorni.com. The Giant's Causeway and the Carrick-a-rede rope bridge are two of the most visited tourist attractions on the north Antrim coast (see chapter: Cycling - Antrim coast).

Best time to go/season:

You can blokart all year round if you have access to open, firm, flat land and enough wind. Wind strength depends on your weight and the surface you are using. A child will get going in as little as 5 kts of wind, whereas an adult will need about 8–10 kts. The rougher the surface the more wind you will need. If you are blokarting on the beach you will need to check tide times and wind direction and ensure the sand is firm enough to blokart on.

Links:

www.blokarters.com

www.kitecrew.co.uk

www.blokart.com

www.theblsa.com

(British land and speed sail association)

www.blokartheaven.co.nz

www.ipksa.info

(Irish power kite and sandyacht association)

www.blokart.co.uk.

MOUNTAIN BOARDING
MOURNE MOUNTAINS, CO. DOWN

I arrived for an afternoon session (2 p.m.) at the Surfin' Dirt mountain board centre in the Mourne mountains. Two teenage boys were just finishing their introductory session. The pair were a real advertisement for the sport, both beaming from ear to ear. The younger of the two was so taken by his session that he had invested in a second-hand board. His investment ensures he only pays £10 per day for all future visits. For the owner Gary Parr, it's not about making money but encouraging people to get involved in the sport – having more boarders makes for better competitions.

Competitions like 'king of the dirt' take place on dirt tracks or forest runs. Pairs of boarders compete, with one being knocked out in each race. Survival of the fittest. The Irish Open Mountain Boarding Championship includes boardercross, giant slalom and freestyle competitions. Injuries at the Surfin' Dirt track are very rare. The injuries tend to

occur when boarders are unfamiliar with the terrain.

Gary himself instructs beginners; he also runs training courses for those interested in becoming instructors (over sixteen) in which he trains participants to deliver Level 1 beginners tuition. Trainees need to pass the All Island Mountain Boarding Association (AIMBA) instructor practical assessment, after which they will be listed as approved AIMBA instructors.

My lesson began with kitting out in obligatory safety gear – helmet, wrist guards, elbow and knee pads. Gary accompanied me to the nursery slope, where he explained how mountain boarding compares to snowboarding: 'easier to learn, harder to fall.' He gave me a very comprehensive introduction to the sport. My limited surfing and snowboarding experience did stand to me and I picked up the basics quickly. Gary gauged my ability well and moved through a series of progressions. While I was only practising turns and emergency stops on the nursery slope I enjoyed the challenge. The safety gear gave me the confidence to try Gary's tips. I finished my lesson with some boarding over a few mounds and while still on the lower slopes it definitely got the adrenaline going. My session did leave me wanting more and I will be back for a longer (perhaps even full-day) session. I regretted not being able to get a run on the dirt track higher up in the mountain but my skills wouldn't have taken me there after just one introductory session. I had the entire course to myself as it was a quiet day; Gary explained that the board owners come out to play on the weekends. The course is dotted with mounds, ramps and rails for the more experienced boarders. There was one white-knuckle ramp which I initially assumed was for advertising purposes – not so. Apparently the extreme boarders will give anything a go. It was about a 20–30 foot climb up a couple of ladders and then a virtually sheer drop onto the ramp below – not for the faint hearted. I admired it from a distance.

I did feel part of the attraction of 'Surfin' Dirt' was the dirt and while my ass was respectably grass and mud-streaked after practising my emergency stops I lacked that feeling of having gotten really down and dirty. For those that do get sufficiently mucky Surfin' Dirt offers a 'surf, soak and stay' package with nearby accommodation. Surf the mountain, soak in seaweed baths and stay overnight surrounded by the dramatic scenery of the Mourne mountains.

Getting there:

By Car:
Surfin' Dirt is situated between the villages of Bryansford and Kilcoo in Co. Down, N. Ireland, on the Tullyree Road.

Travelling from Belfast:
Leave the city on the A24 towards Carryduff, Ballynahinch and Newcastle. At Clough turn right onto the A25 towards Castlewellan. In the town of Castlewellan turn left at the roundabout onto the A50 for Newcastle. 3 km along, turn right onto the B180 towards Bryansford and Hilltown. Once through the village of Bryansford, take the second road to the right, which is signposted for Kilcoo. The Surfin' Dirt track is 200 yards along on the right.

Travelling from Newry:
Leave the city taking the B8 for Hilltown and Newcastle. Travelling through Mayobridge and Hilltown, continue until the end of the B8. Turn right at the T-junction towards Kilcoo. In Kilcoo, you will see a fork in the road, just past the church on the left. Keep to the right; this is the Tullyree Road, which you should follow to the end. As you reach the forest at the end of the road, you will see the Surfin' Dirt track on the left.

The area:
Surfin' Dirt is located at the foot of the Mourne mountains. The twelve peaks of the Mourne mountains include Slieve Donard, which at 850

metres is Northern Ireland's highest mountain. The Mourne Wall is among the most famous feature in the Mourne mountains. The very distinctive Mourne Wall is a dry stone wall that runs for 35 km and crosses fifteen summits. The wall was constructed to define the land purchased by the Belfast Water Commissioners in the late 1800s. For more information about the area check out www.mournemountains.com.

Provider:

There is currently only one centre in Ireland, nestled in the heart of the scenic Mourne mountains in Co. Down. Owned and run by the enthusiastic Gary Parr, Surfin' Dirt is open to all, from beginners to extreme boarders. Beginners have the opportunity to learn and develop skills on the nursery slope, while more advanced riders will enjoy the long carving runs, and jumps on the main course. The track is open Saturdays 10.30 a.m. to 6 p.m. and Sundays from 12 noon to 6 p.m. Beginners' training sessions cost £15, last for three hours and begin at 11 a.m. and 2 p.m. on Saturdays and 2 p.m. on Sundays. Prices include board and safety gear. Returning riders pay £7 for one hour and £12 for two hours.

A seven-hour all-day hire session costs £25. Board owners can 'ride all day' for £10.

For more information check out www.surfindirt.co.uk, +44 (0)77 3921 0119 or email Gary at gary@surfindirt.co.uk

More about Mountain Boarding:

Mountain boarding is one of a new wave of adventure activities surfacing in Ireland. Now is the time to get involved. Surfin' Dirt is an accessible, affordable introduction to the adrenaline sport of mountain boarding.

This sport originated when snow was a little too thin on the ground for snowboarders. It soon developed into a bona fide sport which now boasts its own governing body, the All Island Mountain Boarding Association (AIMBA).

Accommodation:

For accommodation options in the Mourne mountain area check out the accommodation section on www.mournemountains.com or www.discovernorthernireland.com. You can also contact the Newcastle tourist information centre at +44 (0)28 4372 2222.

Other attractions:

There are plenty of activities in the area, including hill walking, cycling, climbing, golf, horse riding and fishing. The Mourne mountains are a popular climbing location; for a list of climbs in the mountains check out www.climbing.ie or www.mournesclimbers.com. Moneyscalp wood, about 1 mile from Bryansford village, has a challenging downhill off-road mountain biking trail; see www.nimountainbiking.com. For more information on outdoor activities in Northern Ireland check out www.outdoorni.com.

Best time to go/season:

The track is open all year round. Bad weather conditions can stop play, so phone before travelling if conditions look poor.

Links:

www.surfindirt.co.uk

www.mournemountains.com

www.outdoorni.com

www.mbseurope.com.

CYCLING ANTRIM COASTLINE, CO. ANTRIM

We set off from Portstewart at 8.30 a.m. on a 70 km cycle along the famous causeway coastal road. A short spin dominated by golf courses and long sandy beaches took us through Portrush, a popular seaside resort, and on to our first stop, Dunluce castle. The impressive castle ruins stand perched on top of a high cliff edge set against the rugged Antrim coastline. Apparently Michael Jackson tried to buy the castle a few years ago.

We took a few minutes to appreciate the view before setting off again. There is nothing as frustrating or perplexing as a headwind that seems to change direction with you. Whenever we felt respite was coming, the wind lashed into our faces and made us work hard. The next stop on the route was Bushmills, home of the world's oldest distillery. Bushmills single malt whiskey was first produced here in 1608. We skipped the distillery tour, deciding the time would be better spent at the Giant's Causeway.

The Giant's Causeway is one of those places you hear about but are never prepared for. It is breathtaking. The headlands, majestic cliffs and inaccessible bays all frame the incredible rock formations which the area is famed for. We left the bikes under the watchful eye of the security guards at the gates and walked the short path down to the massive polygonal black columns jutting out of the sea. The causeway was formed over sixty-two million years ago after a long period of igneous activity. The fast cooling caused cracking and created the fascinating hexagonal columns we were walking on, an incredible 40,000 or so of them. The dramatic site has inspired one of Ireland's best legends. The story goes that mythical Irish giant Finn MacCool built the causeway to get to Scotland and battle with a rival giant called Benandonner. When he got there he found that the Scottish giant was asleep but also far bigger than himself, so Finn returned back across the causeway. When Benandonner woke he came across the causeway, intent on fighting Finn. Finn's wife dressed up her husband as a baby and when Benandonner arrived she said Finn wasn't home and to be quiet so as not to wake the baby. When Benandonner saw the 'baby' he decided that if the baby was that big, Finn must be massive. Afraid of being defeated he fled back across the causeway, ripping it up as he went. All that remained were the two ends, the Giant's Causeway and a similar formation on the island of Straffa in Scotland. The legend tells us that one of the lumps of earth left a hole that filled with water; this became Lough Neagh. Another lump landed in the sea; today we call it the Isle of Man. Sufficiently impressed, we walked the high coastal path back to the visitor centre and set off along a magnificent stretch of coastline that includes Dunserverick castle, White Park bay and the Carrick-a-Rede rope bridge.

We reached Carrick-a-Rede in no time. We paid £3 to gain access to the 1 km walkway down to the famous rope bridge. The narrow swinging rope bridge hovers 80 feet above the sea and connects the mainland to a small offshore Island. Traditionally, fishermen erected the bridge to Carrick-a-Rede Island to check their salmon nets. The bridge has been stabilised in recent years and as a result was much sturdier than I had imagined. A queue had formed, which gave us the opportunity to watch as numerous people chickened out at the last minute. No-one has ever been injured falling from the bridge but there are apparently many instances of visitors being unable to face the return walk across the bridge, resulting in them being taken off the island by boat. We took in the stunning views of Rathlin and the Scottish Islands before making our way back to the bikes and starting into a gruelling climb from the car park. The downhill descent into Ballycastle came as a welcome relief.

The road out of Ballycastle seemed to climb indefinitely. We struggled all the way, taking turns leading the battle against the strong head winds that plagued us since setting off from Portstewart. The wind was so strong against us we needed to change to a lower gear going downhill.

We only had thirty minutes to reach Cushendall to catch the bus back to Portstewart, and according to our calculations we were facing into another steep climb before arriving in Cushendall. We stopped at a petrol station for some food to sustain us on our climb. We asked the shopkeeper how far to Cushendall. He said: 'You're in Cushendall.' Happy days.

We had miscalulated the route allowing us enough time to catch a quick bite to eat in Mc-Collam's restaurant before taking the last bus of the day back to Portstewart. A challenging but rewarding cycle along spectacular coastal scenery.

Getting there:

Portstewart is approx. four and a half hours' drive from Dublin and just over an hour from Belfast. From Dublin take the N1 north to Dundalk. From there take the A1 north to the M1 (signposted Belfast) and then the M2 (signposted Ballymena). From Ballymena take the A26 to Coleraine. If driving from Derry take the A6 to Coleraine and follow signs for PortStewart. For a detailed route plan check out the route planner on www.aaroadwatch.ie.

Northern Ireland's transport service, Translink (www.translink.co.uk, +44 028 90 66 66 30) runs a regular express bus and rail service between Dublin, Belfast, Derry and Coleraine; you then catch a bus to Portstewart. Bikes are carried free of charge on the train, although there are restrictions.

There are direct flights to Belfast international airport from nearly all major UK airports, many European cities, the US and Canada. Northern Ireland also has great ferry connections with Scotland, England and the Isle of Man.

The area:

This coastal road takes in some of Northern Ireland's most impressive scenery.

Dunluce castle (www.northantrim.com) was built by Richard de Burgh, the earl of Ulster. In 1584 it fell to the battle hardy MacDonnell clan who ruled this northeastern corner of Ireland in the sixteenth century. In 1588 the MacDonnells used treasure from the Spanish Armada ship, the *Girona*, wrecked off the Giant's Causeway, to refurbish the castle. However, in 1639 during a violent storm, a portion of the castle's kitchen, along with some of the cooks, fell into the sea. After this the castle was abandoned by the MacDonnells. Tours available Easter to September;

out of season tours also available. Booking is advised. Adults: £2, children under four: free.

The Giant's Causeway (www.giantscauseway-centre.com) is Ireland's top tourist attraction and only UNESCO world heritage site.

The unusual six-sided basalt columns were formed by volcanic activities during the Tertiary period fifty–sixty million years ago. Specialist group guided tours operate June to August (booking necessary – phone +44 (0)28 2073 1855 for prices). Access to the stones and coastal path is free and open all year round.

Bushmills distillery tours (www.bushmills.com) operate from April to October: Mon–Sat 9.30 a.m to 5.30 p.m., Sun noon to 5.30 p.m., last tour 4 p.m; November to March: seven-day opening but reduced tours. Phone +44 (028) 2073 3218 for tour times.

Adult £5, child £2.50, concession £4, family £13.

The Carrick-a-Rede rope bridge (www.nationaltrust.org.uk) is open, weather permitting, from:

1 Mar–27 May: 10 a.m.–6 p.m. daily
28 May–2 Sep: 10 a.m.–7 p.m. daily
3 Sep–31 Oct: 10 a.m.–6 p.m. daily

Adult: £3 child: £1.50, family: £7.50, group: £2.30pp.

Rathlin Island: The ferry to Rathlin Island travels just ten kilometers across the 'sea of Moyle'. This island is 7 km long, 4km wide and home to around seventy people, a seal colony and numerous birds (puffins, guillemots, razorbills and kittiwakes). On clear days Donegal, the north Antrim coastline, the island of Islay and the Mull of Kintyre can be seen. Phone +44 (028) 2076 9299 for ferry information.

Provider:

Bike Rental: The nearest places to rent bikes are Coleraine (G McAlister Cycles, +44 (0)28 7034 4704, 16 Glenleary Road, Coleraine) and Bushmills (The Bushmills Bike Company, +44 (0)28 207 30262; + 44 (0)79 6691 3682, The Shop, 140 Main Street, Bushmills)..

If you're travelling from Belfast you can rent bikes at Life Cycles (www.lifecycles.co.uk, +44 (0)28 9043 9959, 36–37 Smithfield Market, Belfast), McConvey Cycles (www.mcconveycycles.com, +44 (0)28 9033 0322, 183 Ormeau Road, Belfast) or Bike Dock (www.bikedock.com, + 44 (0)28 9073 0600, 79–85 Ravenhill Road, Belfast).

More about Cycling:

This is a busy tourist road and traffic can be quite heavy, especially during the summer months. Bring warm, wind- and rainproof clothing and comfortable walking shoes for getting to some of the tourist attractions. There are plenty of towns to stop at along the way for food and drink.

For a list of other cycling routes in Northern Ireland check out the Cycle Northern Ireland website (www.ncn-ni.com).

For a comprehensive list of cycling clubs in Ireland check out the club directory on www.cyclingireland.ie

The map displays an alternative route via Torr

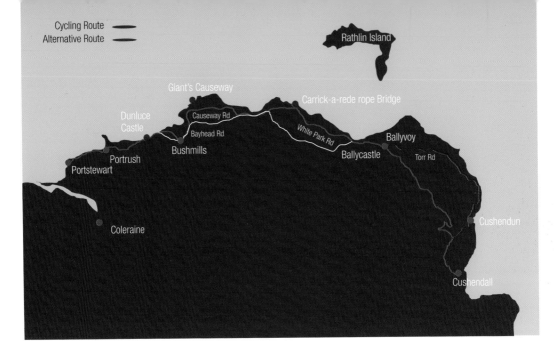

Cycling Route ━━
Alternative Route ━━

Rathlin Island

Giant's Causeway

Carrick-a-rede rope Bridge

Dunluce
Castle

Causeway Rd

White Park Rd

Ballyvoy

Bayhead Rd

Ballycastle

Torr Rd

Bushmills

Portrush

Portstewart

Cushendun

Coleraine

Cushendall

head. One particular part of this route is up an un-rideable steep section.

Accommodation:

For cycle-friendly accommodation try Cul-erg House B&B, Portstewart (+44 (0)28 7083 6610, 9 Hillside, Portstewart), Juniper Hill caravan park (+44 (0)28 7083 2023, 70 Ballyreagh Rd, Portstewart), Carrick Dhu caravan park (+44 (0)28 7082 3712, 12 Ballyreagh Rd, Portrush), Rick's Causeway Coast hostel (+44 (0)28 7083 3789, 4 Victoria Terrace, Portstewart), Chez-Nous (+44 (0)28 7083 2608, 1 Victoria Terrace), Craigmore House (+44 (0)28 7083 2120, 26, The Promenade, Portstewart), O'Malley's Edgewater hotel (+44 (0)28 7083 3314, 88 Strand Rd, Portstewart) or Comfort hotel, Portrush (+44 (0)28 7082 6100, Portrush). For more accommodation options in Northern Ireland check out the www.discovernorthernireland.com website.

Other attractions:

The Antrim coast is one of the most visited parts of Northern Ireland. There are numerous activities in the area. The long sandy blue flag beaches along the Antrim coast host a variety of watersports. The Antrim coastline is particularly good for sea kayaking and surfing. White park bay, Portballintrae beach, white rocks and Portrush beach are popular surfing locations. For more activity possibilities check out www.outdoorni.com.

Best time to go/season:

Weekdays in the late spring or early autumn are probably best. This is Northern Ireland's most popular region for tourists, so roads, attractions and accommodation can be unbearably busy on mid-summer weekends and during holidays.

Links:

www.cycleni.com
www.causewaycoastandglens.com
www.outdoorni.com.